BULLIED TO DEATH?

A Story of Bullying, Social Media, And The Suicide of Sherokee Harriman

JUDITH A YATES

WILDBLUE
P R E S S

WildBluePress.com

BULLIED TO DEATH published by:

WILDBLUE PRESS
P.O. Box 102440
Denver, Colorado 80250

WILDBLUE PRESS is registered at the U.S. Patent and Trademark Offices.

ISBN 978-1-947290-45-7   Trade Paperback
ISBN 978-1-947290-44-0   eBook

Interior Formatting/Book Cover Design by Elijah Toten www.totencreative.com

DEDICATION

For Sherokee Rose Harriman
and the countless other children who struggle daily
with too many issues far too early in life.

Bullied To Death? is not a fictionalized version of the death of Sherokee Rose Harriman. The narrative is based on thousands of hours of interviews, social media research, cell phone record research, and review of documentation including police reports, legal transcripts, photographs, media, court reports, and proven resources. All persons are real, but some names and physical descriptions have been changed for reasons of privacy. Although this is a work of nonfiction, some conversations are based upon multiple interviews and records because no verbatim record exists. Alterations are as miniscule as possible in order to remain true to the story. Some people refused to be, or could not be, involved; therefore, their involvement is based on numerous sources that include the recollections of other persons who were involved as well as additional research, and all material was carefully reevaluated for accuracy. The dates, places, and timeline of events are true.

Social media posts are written as they originally appeared, without corrections to spelling or grammar, in an effort to remain true to the story.

Throughout this project, I spoke with young people dealing with suicide; loneliness; depression; self-mutilation; dysfunctional home life; financial difficulties that get in the way of the most basic of needs; verbal, physical, and sexual abuse; bullying; and too many other challenges to list here— all before celebrating their sixteenth birthday. I always left these interviews with one question: how do we, as a society, come to this?

A percentage of book sales will benefit a national nonprofit organization which focuses on the education about and prevention of teen suicide. The donation will be in memory of Sherokee Harriman. If one child can be saved, if one child suicide can be stopped, Sherokee's death was not in vain.

—Judith A. Yates

ACKNOWLEDGMENTS

This book would not be possible without the assistance of the friends and family, law enforcement officials, and those who best knew Sherokee Harriman.

A very special thank you to Sherokee's family for their bravery in their willingness to share all, both good and bad, to better tell Sherokee's story. Your words will help save another child and their family.

And, as always, to my family.

Table of Contents

SEPTEMBER 5, 2015: MANKIN PARK

"When I was a child I spoke as a child; I
understood as a child and I thought as a child."
1 Corinthians 13:11

CHAPTER 1

"Hey bitch, you're a ho!" Later, different people would attribute this shouted challenge to thirteen-year-old Allie Trace.

The focus of Allie's outburst, Sherokee Harriman, stood staring at Allie and the three teens with her. They approached Sherokee at a street corner under a stop sign across the street from Mankin Park, the teen's gathering spot. If a teen was not old enough to drive, there were few other places to go in the small town of LaVergne, Tennessee.

Sherokee, at 14, was not prone to physical fighting. At 5-foot, 3-inches tall and 120 pounds, with a soft complexion and baby face, she did not look exactly intimidating. She tried to keep her lower lip from trembling, shifting her weight from side to side. In a nervous gesture, she pushed a lock of her short, dark hair away from her young face.

"You bitch!" Allie shouted. Pretty in an earthy sense, now Allie's face was pinched in anger. "I'm tired of you saying shit about me!"

The two boys and one girl who accompanied Allie could only stare, eyes wide. Just a few minutes ago when Allie had told them that she wanted to walk over and talk to Sherokee, they had no idea it would lead to this.

"Who are you? You don't even know me!" Sherokee found her voice. "You don't know who I am!"

The boys could not believe it. Girl fights usually made for a cool show, but this was crazy. One moment they were hanging at the park's pavilion, the next they were witnessing an ugly verbal attack. Allie's best friend Debi Hornsby was usually smiling, but now she nervously crossed her skinny arms.

Alec Seether crossed his arms, too, looking from his current girlfriend, Allie, to his ex-girlfriend, Sherokee. One of the kids who stood next to him, Donny Duroy, wondered briefly what Alec was thinking, watching a little girl being attacked, a girl with whom Alec once shared secrets.

"I don't even know you," Sherokee replied. "I've never said anything about you."

"Yeah, you talk about me behind my back!" Allie was not letting up. "But when you can say it to my face, what happens, fucking bitch!"

"I never said anything about you!" Sherokee voice was louder. "I don't even know who you are!"

"Bitch!"

"You better watch it or I'll kick your ass!" Sherokee bravely challenged.

Their voices rose with bravado and the angry exchanges.

A few of the teens would later report to authorities and confide in friends that Debi, the other teen witness, added to the fray by calling Sherokee names. Later, when it was far too late, Debi would deny it.

"He doesn't want you!" Allie was shouting now. "And you better stop talking about me, you ho!"

Debi would later say she tried to get Allie to stop. "Allie! Let's go. Let's just go!"

"You just better watch it, bitch!" Allie shouted at Sherokee.

"You need to shut your fucking mouth!" Sherokee had enough of this bitch with the attitude. She could only be pushed so far.

Alec could not find his voice. He had no idea what to say or do. He knew Allie was mad; she had probably heard the rumor that he was planning to break up with her, maybe return to Sherokee. Earlier, he had told Allie to not start anything when they saw Sherokee approach the park. Now Allie was verbally attacking Sherokee, and it looked like it may go further.

Both Allie and Sherokee were balling up their fists to physically fight, then at the same time, they seemed to abandon the plan. Their fingers uncurled.

Two younger people watched the exchange from a distance: Alec's sister Angelique and Angelique's friend Micky. The younger Micky took off running away from the park. Angelique soon followed. "Where you going, Micky?" one of the boys shouted at her retreating figure.

Now Sherokee was turning on one heel to head away from the group. Her family lived nearby, less than three blocks away. Sherokee often walked to the park, usually to be alone with her thoughts. But today was different.

"Yeah, get out of here, ho!" Allie called after her. "Bitch!"

The teens turned to walk back across the street to Mankin Park. As they settled in the bench seats to sit under the pavilion, someone turned up their cell phone volume to listen to music. Debi checked her own phone for what must have been the hundredth time that day, sometimes lifting it over her head; still, she could not get a signal. She could never get cell phone service in this park, which annoyed her.

She was unaware of how, in just a few minutes, reception would be a matter of life or death.

CHAPTER 2

A furious Sherokee Harriman walked alone down Mankin Street and took a right turn at the corner toward home. She headed for the neat, square, one-story brick home where she lived with her family: her mother, stepfather, an older sister, and her maternal grandmother. As she walked, she decided she would return to the park. She would teach them a good lesson.

She would show them how much they were hurting her, what their words did to her, and then—then—she might only hurt for a little time, but they would be forever harmed.

Sherokee punched numbers into her cell phone to call a friend, Abraham Ringgold, who was her age. Abe and Sherokee had "dated" in elementary school, which consisted of calling themselves "boyfriend and girlfriend" and passing notes in the hallway. Now they attended the same school and rode the same bus, but they had drifted apart in separate lives, only chatting on occasion.

"Can you come to the park?" Sherokee asked Abe.

"I can't ride my bike," he told her ruefully. "I broke my arm. It's too far to walk."

Sherokee told him there were some people in the park, and they were making fun of her.

Then a text message came across her cell phone from her mother, Heather Edwards. Earlier, from work, Heather had given Sherokee permission to leave the house and go to the park, but only if Sherokee would text her every five minutes to let her mom know she was safe. So at 12:09 p.m.[1], not having received a note, a text message appeared:

Hey, its been way longer than 5 minutes, are you alright?

Sherokee put Abe on hold to text back. She punched the keyboard of her cell phone:

Yea sorry

Heather responded:

It's OK. I just don't want anything to happen to you is all.

Sherokee often shared the ups and downs of her life with her mom, and now she confided in her:

I hate this

Heather was busy, but she paused long enough to text back and see what was wrong with her youngest child:

You hate what

It was several minutes before Sherokee's response appeared:

My life

And in a few minutes she added:

I hate being the one to get called a hoe

---

1. Social media posts are written as they originally appeared, without correcting spelling or grammar, in an effort to remain true to the story.

Heather was sighing and shaking her head. In her eyes, it seemed someone was always calling Sherokee names, making fun of her. Heather was tired of these mean kids, tired of a school that she felt turned a blind eye to her complaints and problems with bullies. She texted:

Who's called you a hoe?

Sherokee did not know Allie. They did not attend the same high school nor socialize in the same circles. So, she replied:

Some girl that doesn't even know me

Seconds later, at 12:44 p.m., she texted Heather to let Heather know she was safe:

I'm home

Sherokee was still on the phone with Abe, and they talked about the bullying kids.

Shyloe Harriman looked up from her perch on the couch when her younger sister came into their home, cell phone clamped to one ear as always. Sherokee seemed upset. She stopped to ask Shyloe, "Is granny in the kitchen?"

"No," Shyloe told her, standing up to follow her.

"Good!" She was mad, Shyloe could tell by her tone. But then, Sherokee—her little "Sissy"—always seemed to be mad. Shyloe sat back down. Best to leave her alone.

Sherokee took the few steps into the kitchen, shedding the white down-jacket she wore over her blouse, clothing she had carefully selected only an hour before. She was wrapping the arms of her jacket around her waist, tying the sleeves together at her waistband as she entered the small kitchen.

Shyloe heard her sister rummaging through kitchen drawers.

Four minutes after she had received Sherokee's text about being home, Heather texted Sherokee, asking:

When did she call you that?

Shyloe walked outside to lounge on the front steps as her sister left the house. "I'm going to the park," Sherokee told Shyloe, storming out the front door.

Shyloe did not reply. She had no idea what was going on, but it was not difficult to see Sherokee was, once again, mad about something.

Abe listened to the silence on the phone after Sherokee told him, "Hold on, my mom's texting me again."

As she worked, Heather Edwards picked up her cell phone to see another text from her daughter at 12:48 p.m.:

I'm going back to the park hopefully they r not there

Heather texted Sherokee the same thing she always said when girls bullied her pretty daughter:

So it was said to you today. Baby girl, that girl is just jealous, cause you are prettier than her

But this time she has no idea if Sherokee read it.

Sherokee was back on the phone with Abe. "Okay, I'm here."

Abe made a few comments, but there was no reply.

Sherokee was walking back to Mankin Park, casually, her heart pounding. She touched the item hidden in her jacket. It felt surreal, but it also seemed to be so natural. Like breathing, or walking, maybe. She was going to show them. She was going to scare them and scare them good, let them see what mean words and names can do to a person.

And maybe, after they learned their lesson, she could be their friend.

If not, they would hurt forever. And at least maybe her pain would not last, not squeeze her heart in pangs of sadness.

The next thing she said to Abe was, "I have a knife."

CHAPTER 3

Abe could not speak for a moment, then he found his voice. "What are you going to do?" he demanded. "Sherokee, whatever you're going to do, don't do it, okay?" He waited. "Please!"

"I'm going back to the park."

"Please!" Abe felt hot tears in his eyes. He could envision Sherokee waving the knife at her tormenters, or maybe she would actually walk up to them with a knife. What if she stabbed one of the bullies? What if she stabbed herself? At the same time, he told himself, *No. That is so not her. It just is not in her to even* hold *a knife!*

Abe was still shouting into the phone. "Sherokee! Sherokee! Whatever you're going to do, don't do it, okay?" Panic was riding in his throat now. *She is going to get into big trouble. Why does she have a knife? She's not going to hurt anybody ... oh God, what if she hurts somebody?* "Please—no—Sherokee!"

Crossing Mankin Street to the park, Sherokee saw Allie sitting at the table under the pavilion with Alec, the other boy, and the girl. Without knowing who they were, Sherokee saw Angelique and Micky had returned, sitting with the group of older kids. Two bicycles rested casually against the benches. They were all laughing and talking, the girls flipping their hair over their shoulders. When someone pointed out Sherokee's return, Allie turned in her seat. She watched her target approach them along the paved path.

Sherokee stopped just past the park entrance. There was a slight smile, a Mona Lisa-type expression on her face. Her hand slipped into the folds of her jacket, fishing for something. She brought it out to clasp in both hands.

The kids just stared at her.

Sherokee looked them over. "So you think it's funny to call me a ho and a bitch?" she shouted.

She raised her fists, clamped together, over her head. Then she swung them, hard, back over her head to punch herself in the gut.

Debi would later say that she witnessed it all. She also reports that she, Alec, and Donny were talking over the music when they heard Allie scream, "You guys! I need your help!"

"I turned and saw Allie beside Sherokee, who was lying on the ground," Debi explains. "And we ran over to her."

Alec would later report he was the first one to Sherokee as she collapsed into the grass.

Abraham Ringgold says now, "It got quiet, then I started hearing people screaming, 'Call 911! Call 911!' Then the phone shut off."

There are conflicting reports about what took place in Mankin Park that day, but one detail remains the same: Sherokee Harriman was now lying on her back, moaning, a kitchen knife plunged into her stomach.

CHAPTER 4

LaVergne officials like to say their town is "the heart of middle Tennessee." According to their statistics, the city is ranked sixth in the state for being "business friendly" and is the fourth best place in Tennessee to find low property taxes and utility bills.

LaVergne is a comparatively young town, incorporated in 1972, despite it being christened in 1852 after Francois Lenard Gregoire de Roulhac de LaVergne. The postmaster at the time just called it "LaVergne."

Located in Rutherford County, the town of just over 34,000 is off I-24 East and southeast of "Music City," Nashville. With a median age of 31 years, LaVergne is racially disproportionate with eighty-five percent of its citizens being white. The average household brings home an annual salary of about $50,000. Forty-eight percent of the population lives below the poverty line.

The town boasts several large businesses, including Ingram Book Company and Bridgestone/Firestone. The population is growing, and many people commute from LaVergne and surrounding areas to Nashville. Westbound I-24 becomes a parking lot early weekday mornings. Eastbound after 5 p.m. is just as slow; the thirty-minute drive to and from Nashville stretches into what seems like forever.

Percy Priest Lake is just north of LaVergne, a great place for weekend boaters to throw out their fishing lines or just enjoy the water, their voices carrying over to the shorelines.

For fun, there are several parks dotting the city landscape, including Mankin Park on Mankin Street off of Jefferson Pike, a busy two-lane road. The park sits in the middle of a quiet suburban area where neighbors take pride in their small homes. Mankin Park is well maintained, its grass clipped and trees pruned and mulched. Children can swing on the big, green swing set or climb all over the playground with its blue slide and little climbing wall. Plenty of pretending can happen in the fortress-type wooden play set, where little ones can climb up and lord over the wood-chip playground and nearby blankets of leaves. There is also a covered pavilion over three rows of metal picnic tables with attached bench seats.

After September 5, 2015, another attraction came to Mankin Park: a pole near the entrance, wrapped in pink ribbon. It is a memorial of flowers, balloons, cards, and small stuffed animals all clustered together. The cards are addressed to Sherokee Harriman, the 14-year-old child who stabbed herself and fell near that spot.

"DID YOU STAB YOURSELF?"

Sherokee, did you stab yourself in the stomach?

—Text message to Sherokee Harriman from her mother, Heather, September 5, 2015, 1:07 p.m.

CHAPTER 5

Seconds after Sherokee Harriman plunged the knife into her own stomach, she seemed to melt to the ground, landing on her back. Her hands pounded the dirt at her sides; her legs twitched and jerked. She began screaming, withering in pain. The teens at the picnic table ran over to where she lay; they saw the kitchen knife lying near the girl's body, a dot of blood pooling on her shirt just above the bellybutton. "It hurts!" she was able to moan. "It hurts! Ohhhh…"

Allie Trace began applying pressure to the wound using Sherokee's down jacket. Sherokee had almost turned over onto the knife, Allie would later tell officials, so she moved the knife away to prevent further harm. Debi Hornsby was cradling Sherokee's head in her hands. "I didn't want her to hit her head [or] bang it on the sidewalk," she would later explain. Sherokee's head lolled side to side; the girl was moaning, and she was trying to talk. Her breath came in and out, slowly, in deep gasps and slow exhales.

Allie and Debi were talking to her in rapid-fire succession.

"It's okay, Sherokee, you're going to be okay!"

"Just take it easy … we sent for help…"

"Call somebody!" Allie demanded of Debi.

"I can't!" Debi told her. "I don't get a signal here!" She was panicked, but managed to pat Sherokee's hair, smoothing it away from her face, which was growing pale. "It's okay, Sherokee," she whispered as calmly as possible, trying to say the things that first responders would say. "Help will get here soon... just breathe."

Sherokee coughed deeply, and brown bile dribbled over her lips. The bile dripped onto Allie's leg, staining her blue jeans.

Allie was pushing down on the wound, still using Sherokee's jacket to try and stop the bleeding. She tried to call her parents on her cell phone but there was no answer.

At the same time, one of the boys found Sherokee's cell phone lying next to her and was trying to find someone to call. It was difficult to see the names and numbers because the phone had a spider-web crack across the dark screen, with white paint across the cracks. He was scrolling to find a phone number, any number; his hands shook so badly he almost dropped the phone. The first name in the alphabetized phone list was "Angel." He managed to hit the telephone icon to dial this number.

Eighteen-year-old Angel Hollenbeck was on her home computer that Saturday when her cell phone lit up, and she picked it up to see who was calling. The caller ID showed it was Heather Edwards, her friend Sherokee's mom. Despite their age difference of five years, Sherokee and Angel considered themselves to be close friends. "Hello!" she answered.

Instead of Heather's voice, there was a boy on the other end, and he was shouting about Sherokee.

"Wait—hold on—who is this?" Angel demanded.

He was shouting that Sherokee had stabbed herself, and now she was on the ground. "She's bleeding! She's not talking!"

Angel began shouting at the boy that he was calling from Heather's phone, and she was *not* Heather.

"This is the phone Sherokee has!"

A slow panic began to settle into Angel Hollenbeck. "Someone needs to call Heather!" she told him. "Someone needs to call Heather!"

The teens were trying to help Sherokee, but according to the report later filed by the LaVergne Police Department, they also told Angelique and Micky to get out of the park, to go home now. Go home and forget everything they saw.

At the same time, Abraham Ringgold was texting, then calling, his cousin Katie Nichols,, Sherokee's best friend. Katie was at a baby shower for a family member when she answered her cell phone to hear Abe shouting, "You need to go down to the park! Sherokee has a knife and these kids are bullying her!"

Katie had to ask him to repeat himself, and even then she was not sure she believed it. The baby shower was going on around her, and it made it difficult to hear her cousin's voice over the chatter and laughter. Katie hung up on Abe and texted Sherokee as fast as her fingertips could fly across the keyboard.

Please text me cant get to you right now

Heather Edwards, Sherokee's mother, stands just over five feet tall. She is stout, with deep brown eyes and long dark hair. Heather has a ready smile and a soft heart despite her tough appearance. Heather can tell you, like anyone who has had an unexpected family trauma, exactly where she was and what she was doing about 1 p.m. on September 5, 2015.

Heather and her husband Mike had started a housecleaning business and were cleaning the house of a new client, a Mrs. Joy Hendrick, when the text message came across Mike's cell phone.

Whats Heathers number because Sherokee stabbed herself in the stomach

"What the…" he looked at Heather. "It's Angel, and she's wanting your number." He used Sherokee's nickname. "She's saying Chik stabbed herself in the stomach…"

"*Sherokee* stabbed herself?" Heather stopped work, a cleaning rag dangling from her hand, to stare at Mike. "What?"

Heather grabbed her own cell phone and began frantically searching for Angel's phone number. Angel answered immediately.

"I got a call," Angel was telling her, "and they said Sherokee stabbed herself!"

Heather did not believe it. Lately she did not like the way Angel had been treating Sherokee; they were supposed to be best friends, but Heather did not consider Angel much of a friend. She did not like or trust Angel. And teens played stupid pranks. As the mother of two teen girls, she knew what young people were capable of.

"... Mankin Park she's at Mankin Park..."

Heather looked at Mike. "You better get your ass over to Mankin Park and see what's going on," she said as she hung up the phone.

Mike dropped a cleaning rag and headed for his car. He called to Heather, "I'll be back as quick as I can." It was not far from the Hendrick's home to Mankin Park.

Mike was already starting the engine as the driver's door slammed. As he drove away from the home, Mrs. Hendrick passed by on her way home. Listening to the fading roar of the car's engine, Heather now dialed her personal phone, the cell phone Sherokee was carrying this day. It was 12:54 p.m.

The boy on the other end of the line was not laughing. "She stabbed herself! She's just laying here and not moving."

"What?" Heather demanded. "Wait—who is this?"

"Her head's just moving side to side!" The boy was frantic now. "We can't get her to talk..."

"Where are you?"

"We're at the park! Mankin Park..."

She still thought it was a cruel joke. Sherokee had been bullied by kids; perhaps their torment was now focused on Sherokee's family. It did not sound plausible to Heather:

Sherokee was a "drama queen," and she had some problems, but for her to actually take a knife... Just recently her daughter had to be held down by nurses for an emergency IV. She would scream like a banshee if she hurt herself. At 1:07 p.m., Heather hung up the phone and immediately texted her daughter:

Sherokee, did you stab yourself in the stomach?

Back at Mankin Park, Alec and Donny were running to the pavilion for their bicycles to pedal away toward the direction of where Sherokee lived, hoping someone was at home.

Sherokee's maternal grandmother and legal guardian, Rita Harriman, had returned home from visiting a family member. It was just another Saturday. Then there was a frantic pounding at the front door.

Shyloe opened the door to see two boys in their early teens now hopping back on their bicycles at the foot of the porch. She recognized one of the boys; he had dated Sherokee.

What they told her had her screaming for Rita, who grabbed her purse, and told Shyloe to get her shoes and get into the van. Rita had never been to Mankin Park, so she tried to get Shyloe to focus and point out the streets, but the girl became hysterical. Shyloe babbled directions, but in her panic she was not sure where to turn. They drove around a few blocks to finally locate the park. Rita observed the group of teens kneeling and standing around Sherokce, who was lying in the grass.

Rita jerked the van to a halt and hurried over to the group, Shyloe at her heels. A girl was applying pressure to Sherokee's stomach using Sherokee's jacket, but there was no visible blood. Another girl and the boys on the bicycles were just standing around, staring at Sherokee. In Rita's eyes, none of them seemed too upset; there were no tears, no signs of fear. But Rita was slipping into numbness.

Not long after they received the calls and the text messages, Mike was slamming on the brakes, simultaneously leaping out of his car and turning off the engine, and he raced up to Mankin Park. Mike saw a group of teenagers standing around just at the park entrance. When they saw him, they parted. That is when he realized it was no joke: this was serious. Sherokee was lying on the ground, and one of the teens was on her knees at Sherokee's side, applying pressure to a wound on Sherokee's stomach.

"Chik! Chik!" Mike dropped down on his knees to shout at his daughter, grabbing her by the shoulder to shake her. She was not responding, and now her breath was coming in rapid, wet gasps. Mike thought of a fish out of water: her cheeks puffing and her lips puckering. "What happened!" he demanded.

The girl who was applying pressure to Sherokee's wound lifted up the jacket to show Mike the small stab would. There was little blood.

"Has anyone called 9-1-1?" Mike demanded.

"We don't have any minutes on our cellphones," one of the teens said.

He looked at Rita, who was in a daze. "Why didn't you call!"

Rita was in shock. "I don't know the number..." she managed to mumble.

Mike called 9-1-1 on his cell phone, hands shaking.

Rita picked up a kitchen knife she found on the grass and tossed it aside to kneel down. A witness says they heard her say, "Guess we'll have to start hiding the knives again." Rita denies this vehemently.

Sherokee's eyes were open, but she was staring at something no one else could see. She was no longer moaning, and her labored breathing sounded wet and ragged. There was bile and blood around her lips. She was rolling slightly side to side.

The operator's voice at 9-1-1 dispatch seemed so cool and calm. "9-1-1. Police or ambulance?"

"Ambulance!"

"What is your emergency?"

CHAPTER 6

Sherokee's aunt Samantha was at home with her daughters when she received a strange text message from her mother Rita. She tried to make sense of it, but the words seem strung together in nonsensical sentences. She read "Sherokee" and "ambulance." Samantha called her mother. "What happened?" she asked Rita.

"Sherokee stabbed herself," was the reply. Rita shared what few details she had.

Samantha immediately ended the call and dialed her husband Jason at work.

Jason was working at the store where he had clocked in and out for over 10 years. When Jason heard his wife crying into her phone, he immediately clocked out and ran to his car. He made it home in half the usual driving time to pull his wife into his arms.

They told their daughters to stay at home and watch out for one another. Jason and Samantha drove to Rita's little home and in what seemed like seconds were walking through the house, calling for everyone and finding no one.

"Mom said it was at a park near here," Samantha told Jason as she led the way back to their car. But they drove around endlessly, trying to find the park. Samantha was crying, and Jason would reach over to squeeze her shoulder and hand in comfort, his beefy hand gently patting her arm.

LaVergne Police Department Officers Crowder, Shields, and Candle were on the scene at 1:19 p.m. LaVergne Fire Department Officers Whitley and Cole arrived right behind them, parking the big, red truck in the street and immediately going into rescue mode.

Everyone in the neighborhood could hear the cry of the EMS vehicle before they saw it. Mike and Rita hurried to move their vehicles to allow room for the ambulance. The bright red emergency vehicle turned the corner and rolled to a stop on Mankin Street. Paramedics leapt out and hustled over to where Sherokee lay in the grass. Their official time at the scene would be marked as 1:23 p.m.

An investigator noted they observed a "white female... lying on her back at the entrance of the park." There was a brown liquid seeping out of her mouth, and a small amount of blood on her shirt. Carefully lifting the girl's shirt, they observed a puncture wound just above the navel. "What happened?" the investigator asked the cluster of teens nearby. "Did anyone see anything?"

"She stabbed herself with a knife," came one answer.

"We were just sitting there and she stabbed herself."

"I heard her yell."

The investigator asked, "Where's the knife now?"

"I have it." Rita stepped forward.

"Where was it?"

"When I got here it was by her head."

The investigator took the knife from Rita and began to secure it as evidence.

Now Mrs. Hendrick was pulling up in her car, Heather as her passenger. Heather was crying, and her client was consoling her.

Crime scene tape hung around the area, cordoning it off from the bystanders now gathering on the once-quiet street. The onlookers crossed their arms and asked one another for insight. A few stood on tiptoe in an effort to see what was happening.

Sherokee was lifted onto a gurney and placed in the ambulance, carefully but quickly. Rita followed, taking a front seat in the ambulance, twisting in her seat in an attempt to watch the efficient paramedics leaning over Sherokee, working with a calm sense of urgency. The ambulance pulled away, lights throwing color as the siren wailed. It was followed closely by an investigator in his vehicle.

LaVergne Police Department Detectives Stephen Hale and Matt Fracker arrived at the scene around 1:45 p.m., after Sherokee was taken away. Someone briefed them, notebooks out and pens scribbling notes, quietly observing the park, the onlookers, and the teen witnesses who were now sitting or standing apart from one another. They put in a call to crime scene technicians Shields and Keeves.

Photographs were taken for evidentiary purposes, as was Sherokee's jacket. The jacket, smeared with blood and vomit, was bagged for evidence.

Heather and Mike stayed behind to answer law enforcement officer's questions.

The people at the park could still hear the wail of the ambulance as it faded, lifting up and over the city of LaVergne. Inside the ambulance, the scene had turned even more serious.

"I can't get her stabilized!" one of the paramedics was calling out as the ambulance took a turn, forcing the occupants to brace themselves. Rita grabbed the passenger door's handle to steady herself.

Rita called Samantha again. Jason and Samantha were still driving through the neighborhood in a desperate attempt to locate Mankin Park. "They can't get her stabilized," Rita told her daughter. Samantha heard voices in the background. "She's going to have to be life-flighted to Vanderbilt!"

The radio call went out to Vanderbilt Hospital to dispatch the life-flight helicopter. Within minutes, the helicopter was lifting gracefully into the sky, away from downtown Nashville for an eleven-minute flight, where it would meet the ambulance and land in a Methodist church parking lot off busy Nashville Highway. The ambulance pulled up into the parking area to wait.

"Hang with me, sweetheart," the paramedic was telling Sherokee while tearing open bags and jotting down information on a clipboard. "Just hang with me! Sherokee! Can you hear me? Can you hear me?"

They heard the familiar sound of the approaching helicopter, the *whup-whup-whup* of the blades as it angled toward the parking lot.

Rita again dialed her daughter Samantha. She held the cell phone to her ear, heart racing. When Samantha heard her mother's voice through the phone this time, it was calm. "She's not going to make it."

The helicopter flattened the grass at the Methodist church when it landed, causing debris to fly and swirl onto Nashville Highway.

The sound in the ambulance made the paramedic's hair stand on end. *Beeeeeeep…* It was the long, steady tone of a flat line. Their patient's heart had stopped beating.

"No! Come on, honey!" The paramedics began pulling equipment from storage spaces with a controlled sense of urgency. Seconds ticked by. The flat line now changed with the steady sound: *Beep. Beep. Beep…*

"I've got her back!"

Rita was preparing to join the group on their way to the helicopter, but someone took her by the elbow. "I'm sorry, but you can't go on the flight!" They called above the noise. "They'll take care of her! I promise! She's in great hands!"

Besides having a spotless safety record, the life-flight service transports to all Nashville hospitals but has immediate access to Vanderbilt Hospital, which houses the region's only Level I Trauma Center and Children's Hospital. On board, the helicopter carries either two nurses, a nurse and a doctor, or a nurse with the paramedic team. The crew members are dual licensed: they hold either EMT-Paramedic and a nursing license or EMT RN licenses, all multistate. Sherokee truly was in the best hands.

Rita reluctantly joined the investigator in his car, and they drove away, returning to Mankin Park. As they pulled off, the steady *beeeeeeeep* of the flat line sounded again in the ambulance. Then: "She's back! We've got her back!"

Sherokee had to be brought back to life six times before she could be moved to the helicopter.

Now the paramedics, bending forward at the waist and their hair blowing wildly, hurried the gurney toward the chopper as soon as it was safe to transport their patient, and Sherokee was quickly loaded. At 1:49 p.m., the helicopter lifted off and away, toward downtown Nashville to one of the most prestigious hospitals in the United States.

The people on the ground, their hands shielding their eyes, became smaller and smaller as the pilot skillfully pulled up and away.

CHAPTER 7

Back at Mankin Park, Mike and Heather were told their daughter was being life-flighted to Vanderbilt. "But we need you to hang with us here," one of the investigators told them, "to answer a few questions."

Heather told investigators about the text messages and calls she had received. "She goes to LaVergne High School now," Heather told them shakily, "and she was being bullied."

They spoke in low voices. Heather told the investigators that Sherokee was bipolar and suffered PTSD for being sexually abused as a child. Yes, Sherokee was on medication; she was taking Latuda for the bipolar disorder. She showed the investigators her cell phone, displaying the text messages Heather had exchanged with her daughter. The investigators read the messages: the girl had texted she was tired of being picked on, was sad and angered about being the brunt of today's verbal attack, and was returning to the park.

Photographs were taken of the cell phone messages.

Investigators, flipping pages on their pads of paper, rounded up the four teen witnesses still at Mankin Park and had them all sit away from one another. There were two boys and two girls.

A religious family, Samantha and Jason began praying aloud for their niece as their car swooped through the neighborhood, both trying to keep an eye out for traffic and any sign of a city park. Finally, their car screeched to a halt at Mankin Park and both tumbled out of the car. To see beyond the emergency vehicles and crime scene tape, they moved around to the side perimeter of the park where a chain link fence kept them at bay. Samantha saw Rita sitting in the park, her face a blank. "Mom!' She rattled the fence in her hands. "Mom! What happened!"

An officer heard her and stepped over to tell Samantha across the fence, "Ma' am, you can't talk to her right now."

"She's my mother!" Samantha snapped, eyes blazing through tears. "I can talk to my own mother!"

"I'm sorry, but this is an investigation."

"I want to know what's going on!"

The officer apologized again and stepped away.

Meanwhile, Rita sat stoic. An uninformed observer might have thought she was either in a daze or even indifferent. Years of abuse from her late husband had taught Rita that crying is never an option and that showing emotion was forbidden. Her children had learned the same lesson from their bullying father.

Samantha took deep breathes to calm herself, focusing on the park scene. Beyond Rita, the investigators, and the uniformed officers, she saw four young people sitting far apart from one another. One was a young girl who was having some sort of argument with one of the investigators. She was shouting, hands on hips, as if daring the adult.

"Who's that obnoxious kid?" Samantha asked Jason. She saw Heather and Mike sitting at the tables under the pavilion, each smoking cigarettes and looking dazed. Shyloe, crying mightily, was sitting next to them. Heather was holding her close.

Jason stepped behind Samantha and wrapped his burly arms around her, encasing her shoulders now shaking with grief.

Somewhere above in the clear sky, the life-flight helicopter prepared to touch down on the hospital rooftop, its landing as gentle as if it were floating down like a wayward feather. Before the blades slowed, the gurney was out of the doors and the young girl was carted into Vanderbilt Children's Hospital.

Meanwhile, one of Heather's best friends, Amy Duke had just returned from a family day at the lake. Her kids raced into the house giggling and shouting, wet hair plastered to their heads. Amy was telling everyone to get into dry clothes and put wet clothes in a pile when her cell phone chimed, signaling a Facebook message. She mouth dropped open as she read the posts about Sherokee. She hurried the kids back into the car and drove to Mankin Park, her heart pounding. She had known Sherokee for eight years, and the girl was friends with the Duke children.

Mankin Park, usually quiet and unassuming, was now covered with police officers, law enforcement vehicles, first responders, and clusters of neighbors trying to see and sharing what little they knew. Amy learned Sherokee had been taken to Vanderbilt Hospital. Heather was sitting nearby, looking lost and bewildered. Amy could not speak to her good friend: all she could do was stand on the sidelines and stare, surrounded by strangers. Dejected and praying, Amy returned home to stay on Facebook all night, watching for news and reading posts.

"Will you take us to your house, show us where Sherokee's medications are stored?" Detective Fracker asked Heather. Crime scene technician Shields joined them as they spoke.

"Yeah, yeah, sure," Heather told him, stubbing out her cigarette. They made the short trip to the little house Sherokee had departed from just a few hours earlier on her way to the park, hoping friends might join her.

In the small bathroom of her home, Heather showed the officers where Sherokee's medication was kept. A fresh cigarette between her fingers, Heather handed over the prescription bottle of Latuda.

"Can you make sure none of them are missing?"

Heather checked again to ensure the medication was accounted for. She allowed Officer Shields to photograph the pill bottles for evidence.

"Will you see if any other medicines are missing?"

Heather made a complete, quick inventory. No, all of the medicines were accounted for, she told them.

Shields moved on to the kitchen and found a matching set of kitchen knives in a block. Two were missing. Shields' eyes carefully scanned the tiny kitchen, the cabinets, the small table and chairs, the floor. A quick look into kitchen sink revealed one of the knives lying in the sink. Photographs were made of the knives. Satisfied, the investigators returned to Mankin Park.

After answering the investigator's questions, Heather joined Mike and together they returned to the park. They made sure the investigators had no more questions for them before grimly heading to Vanderbilt Hospital.

Crime scene technician Kristine Reeves received the call about 2 p.m. She was told, briefly, about the incident at the park, and she told the team she was on her way. Reeves arrived about forty-five minutes later; as she parked her vehicle, she looked over to see a juvenile male sitting on the base of the park slide. Another juvenile male was sitting at one of the picnic tables under the pavilion, while a female juvenile sat at a separate table.

There was a fourth juvenile, a female standing near the edge of the park. The girl was throwing a rock up into the air, catching it, and tossing it skyward again. The girl was identified as Allie Trace.

Officer Crowder walked over to Reeves, and they greeted one another; Crowder briefed her as they stepped away from her car. Reeves observed Detective Hale speaking with one of the juveniles. "Shields is working the crime scene," Crowder explained. "The girl's jacket and the knife are tagged and bagged."

"Okay." Reeves was taking her own notes. Allie Trace meandered over, hovering nearby.

"This girl here," Crowder pointed out Allie, "she—"

"Wait a minute," Reeves said. "She needs to sit away from us; she doesn't need to hear our conversations."

Allie was moved to inside of the park, but away from the others. She plopped down underneath a tree.

Crowder then continued. "She used the girl's jacket to try and stop the bleeding. The kids say this little girl threw up after she stabbed herself, so we've taken samples."

Reeves thanked the officer and walked over to greet Detective Hale. "I want to take pictures of each of these kids," she told him. "And if they have any marks or blood or anything on them, I'll get that, too."

"Good," Hale agreed. "Kristine, the stories about the knife don't exactly match."

"Well, let's get parental permission to get DNA samples from each of them," she said as she jotted more notes.

Rita, sitting nearby, overheard this conversation. She bit her lip, shifting her seat on the bench. "The kid's stories don't match," she told herself. It was something she held onto later, like a talisman, when it was all over.

CHAPTER 8

Reeves walked over to the girl sitting at a picnic table. The delicate-looking young lady told Reeves that her name was Debi Hornsby. When Reeves took photographs of Debi, including her hands, shoes, and the bottoms of her shoes, Reeves noticed a small cut on Debi's upper left arm. She photographed the cut without measurements, then placed a small ruler next to the cut and took another photograph. If any of the other witnesses had wounds, Reeves wanted those photographed as well, as they may be pertinent to the investigation.

Reeves moved to the boy who sat at the table and spoke softly with him. She took a photograph of him, as Detective Fracker stood nearby.

"Can you take your jacket off for us, son?" Detective Fracker asked the boy, who complied.

Reeves thanked the boy and took a photo of him without his jacket, then photographed the boy's hands, shoes, and the bottoms of both shoes.

Reeves walked over to the second boy, who was sitting on the slide. They spoke, and her camera's shutter clicked again: hands, shoes, and the bottoms of both shoes.

Alec's sister Angelique, along with their mother, Nance Seether, arrived at the scene. CST Reeves also looked over Angelique for evidence, then photographed her, as well as her hands, shoes, and the bottoms of both shoes. Angelique told investigators what she had observed. "[She] stated that her brother and the others told her not to say anything," the police report would read.

Reeves finally approached Allie, who was still sitting under the tree, away from her friends. The investigator spoke to her, then took a set of photographs. The girl was defiant, not happy about having to answer questions. "She threw up, and it got on my leg," Allie told Reeves, showing her a brown stain. Reeves photographed the stain.

Detective Hale asked all of the kids to meet him under the pavilion. By now, some of the parents had arrived, so he asked them to join the group. He carefully explained that the department needed DNA swabs from each child, and each child had to be interviewed again, this time at the police station. The adults gathered each of their children and headed to their separate cars. Debi and Allie were transported in separate police vehicles to the police station; the officers were waiting to hear from their parents.

Once at the station, the Seethers had agreed to a DNA swab, so samples were taken from both Alec and Angelique. The teens were released to their family.

The parents of the other boy, Donny Duroy, arrived, and an investigator spoke with them quietly. They gave consent for a DNA swab to be made, then Donny was allowed to depart the station with his family.

When they questioned Allie, investigators became frustrated with her behavior. Allie would giggle and laugh inappropriately. Perhaps a sign of nervousness? Or something more sinister? One of Allie's friends would later explain, "Allie, she laughs when she gets nervous. I've seen her at school, like if she has to stand in front of the class for a project or something. When she gets nervous, she laughs."

Allie's mother spoke with the investigators by telephone and gave consent to interview and take a test swab from Allie. CST Shields advised the girl of the consent before asking for the DNA sample. Allie repeated that Sherokee had vomited on her, so a sample was taken of the brown bile on Allie's pants leg. Both this sample and the DNA sample were logged into evidence. When Allie's family arrived, they spent some time speaking with her privately in an interview room.

Debi Hornsby's mother arrived and gave consent for DNA testing. Once her evidence was collected, Debi left with her mother.

CST Reeves and CST Shields worked together to carefully log and secure the evidence. Now there were reports to write, notes to compare, and information to be stored for investigative use. It was going to be a long Saturday night.

Because she had handled the knife, Rita Harriman was driven to the police station for elimination fingerprinting. Samantha then drove Rita from the police station to Vanderbilt Hospital with Shyloe in tow. Upon arrival, they were instructed to take seats in the hospital waiting room. Mike and Heather burst through the entrance doors and located their family, their thoughts whirling uncontrollably. There were so many questions and not nearly enough answers.

Heather and Mike found themselves going out of the hospital to light cigarettes and puff nervously, with trembling hands that made it difficult to work a lighter and hold it to the tip of the cigarette. They paced the parking lot, watching people come and go, heedless of the drama taking place in one of the operating rooms inside. Heather managed to text message one of her oldest, dearest friends:

I'm at the hospital. Sherokee stabbed herself. It doesn't look good.

Across social media, Sherokee's friends and family shared the scarce information, requesting words of prayer and sending the same. On Twitter, on Facebook, through emails and instant message, news about Sherokee floated through the galaxy of cyberspace.

Alec Seether's cell phone beeped, indicating he had a message. He checked the screen and saw it was Sherokee's best friend, Katie Nichols. She wanted to know if Alec had heard the news.

Alec typed back, letting Katie know he was witness to the stabbing. He tried to help Sherokee, he insisted; he did nothing to her to make her kill herself. *She stabbed herself,* he explained. Then Alec, like everyone else who took part in the day's events, began keeping an eye on social media, too.

Sherokee's friend Taylor Geffre was reading Facebook posts, and what she read forced her to sit back in her chair, mouth slack. People were posting that Sherokee Harriman had stabbed herself in an apparent act of suicide. She added a post to her own Facebook page:

I need urgent prayers and thoughts for my friend and her family please ! I do not want to say the reason for the respect of the family! Thank you !

Taylor pushed her dark bob of hair away from her face as the tears began to fall, plopping down to her computer's keyboard. *She got tired of it all,* Taylor told herself. *She got tired of the bullying and the pattern of her life and did it.*

Taylor, at twenty years of age, was no stranger to suicide attempts and the struggle to be accepted in school. Her family had moved to LaVergne when she was in the sixth grade; she tried to fit in and get attention by acting the goof. It backfired, and the result was no friends. In class, in the halls, Taylor endured hateful remarks and cutting words. She completed "Bully Reports," the forms that were required to report bullying to the school administration. She talked to teachers. Taylor felt as if no one was helping her, as if no one cared. Now not only was she labeled "psycho girl," but "snitch."

The snide remarks and behaviors ruined her one pleasure, playing clarinet in the school band. Add to it all an undiagnosed bipolar disorder and anxiety disorder. Taylor had a history of two suicide attempts: she tried to hang herself when she was 14, and at 15 she tried to overdose on pills. Taylor had read the sad posts that Sherokee had made on Facebook. She noted, when they talked, Sherokee's moods swung from elated to depressed.

Taylor would later share her feelings upon reading about Sherokee's alleged suicide. "I'm so stupid! I saw all the signs. I didn't try to help her. I didn't do anything!" She sobbed, chest heaving, realizing one reason she had reacted so strongly to Sherokee's stabbing: "It could have been me they're all talking about. It could have been me…"

"I saw what she posted on her Facebook," Taylor would later confide in Angel Hollenbeck once they were able to discuss their mutual friend. "Sherokee felt worthless." Internally, she would berate herself: *why didn't I do anything to help her?*

CHAPTER 9

Eleven minutes after the helicopter had departed the LaVergne Methodist Church on Nashville Highway, the doors to the Vanderbilt Hospital operating room burst open with a *whoosh* and in seconds the seasoned team was hooking up IV bags to metal poles, moving trays of instruments to the bedside, and preparing for emergency surgery. Sherokee Harriman was moved from the gurney to the operating table. The delicate surgery began.

The knife had entered the girl's body two inches above the navel. It was plunged in so deep it had nicked the aorta, the main artery that carries oxygenated blood from the heart's left ventricle down to the abdominal area. The girl was bleeding to death.

Thirty minutes after being wheeled into the OR, again the sound no one wants to hear: *beeeeeeeep...* that long, steady tone of a flat line.

EKG pads were placed on Sherokee's body and the call "clear!"

Beep beep beep beep... the flat line returned to life, jumping into peaks and valleys on the screen. Sighs of relief through the face masks, eyes darting to one another in silent thanks across the girl's body.

IV lines were lifted and carried across the body that still fought to live. Sherokee received a dose of Midazolam Hydrochloride syrup, a medication used to sedate pediatric patients. An endotracheal tube was placed into her mouth and down into the trachea, allowing air to pass to the lungs.

The other end of the tube was hooked to a ventilator, forcing Sherokee to breathe. An oro-gastric tube was placed in her mouth, threaded past her tongue down into the stomach so medication and soluble liquids could feed directly into her stomach. Wires were quickly attached while a Foley catheter and left chest tube were inserted. The team worked quickly but carefully, calling out instruments, the patient's condition, and her vital statistics. A hospital wristband was attached to the little girl's slender wrist and various syringes full of life-saving fluids were handed across the unconscious body. An incision was made into the pulmonary pleurae.[2] This procedure, called a thoracotomy, was executed in order to gain access to the thoracic organs (heart, lungs, esophagus, and the thoracic aorta).

A laparotomy was performed, the large incision in the abdominal wall allowing the surgeons access to the abdominal cavity.

Then: *beeeeeeeep…*

They tried to revive the little girl and succeeded again. Hospital records would later show CPR was utilized a total of eight times: six times in the ambulance and twice on the operating table.

But there was too much damage, too much internal bleeding. Vital organs were failing. Sherokee could not breathe on her own. Her body's internal chemicals would not operate alone to support her body, and circulation of the blood would stop unless pushed artificially. There was little to no chance she would ever recover, ever wake up.

In despair, the medical staff was finally forced to put Sherokee on life-support machines. Doctors had done everything they could, but it was in vain. The surgical team looked at each other, then at the floor, angered and disappointed, sad and miserable, but also knowing they had

---

2. The thin sack surrounding the lungs

done everything they could. A human being can only do so much, and modern machines are limited in their power.

One by one members of the team slowly began to place used surgical instruments onto trays; they pushed IV poles back into the corners, rolling up the clear tubes and dropping bloodied gauze into the haz-mat bags. They prepared to take the girl to a room in the Intensive Care Unit, where her vital signs would have to be monitored; her body would have to fight germs and its homeostasis maintained: circulation, fluids, brain activity, and chemical makeup would be measured and controlled by numerous staff, trained specialists, and machines around the clock.

CHAPTER 10

The family was notified when Sherokee was placed in a room in ICU. They were finally allowed to see her, four hours after Sherokee had arrived in the operating room, but protocol restricted who would be allowed in the ICU. Samantha, Jason, and several family members attempted to go in. "No one is allowed," they were told, "unless they are with the legal guardian. Are you her legal guardian?"

"No! But I'm her aunt!" Samantha began heading for the ICU. She was stopped quick.

"You have to be her legal guardian, or with her legal guardian. I'm sorry, but that's the rule."

Samantha was in a zone between hysterical and furious. "She can't be alone!" She insisted. "We have to see her! Please!"

"I'm sorry..."

"A social worker finally helped us," Samantha tells the story now, tears in her eyes and anger in her voice. "She took us in the back way."

Once they were at Sherokee's bedside, the seriousness of the situation escalated quickly. There were renewed sobs and gasps, and eyes filled with new tears. "She had all kinds of tubes in her," Rita would later explain. "In her nose, in her throat. All kinds of machines around her."

Heather walked into the room, nervously pushing her long, dark hair over her shoulders. "I can't stand it!" She blurted, and shoved out of the room. Sometime that evening, she managed to post on her Facebook wall:

It's NOT looking good for my youngest daughter, Sherokee Harriman.

Heather then texted Katie Nichols, telling her that Sherokee had stabbed herself, that the knife had nicked a main artery.
Katie texted back

Are you serious? Are you serious?

Shyloe asked to see Sherokee. "I wanta see Sissy!" She begged. "I wanta see Sissy." Two family members walked the sister into the room where Sherokee lay. When she saw her sister, Shyloe's face blanched, her eyes rolled back, and her knees buckled. She had to be helped out of the ICU room and had cold water splashed on her face.

The doctors conferred with Rita, Sherokee's legal guardian. They discussed Sherokee's condition in low, calm tones.

They explained that, while on life support, Sherokee would be subjected to tubes in her body and dependent on machines to keep her heart pumping, stabilize her bodily fluids and chemicals, and give her nutrition. She may have to have transfusions, surgery, and artificial temporary paralysis for medical procedures. The simplest of functions would be performed by the machines. She would probably never recover, even if her body could withstand the pain, the artificially aided survival, potential stroke and heart attack, and the wear and tear. In addition to the heartache, the financial cost, and the mental and physical long-term damage to her loved ones, Sherokee no longer had any sort of quality of life.

Rita debated. In her mind, Sherokee was still dancing in front of the webcam to a song by one of her heroes, singing along with a popular star. She was asleep on the couch in an awkward position, one that looked like she would need a chiropractor when she woke up. In Rita's mind, Sherokee was setting her hair for church in a style she had studied on YouTube, or arguing about why parental rules were so unjust. She could not imagine Sherokee being unable to move, to dance, to do anyone's hair or nails. Sherokee just lying there with only machines to make her breathe…

Rita finally looked up at the doctor, her eyes bleary behind her glasses. She sighed deeply. "If she has to be on machines to live," her shaking voice cracked, "let her go."

Heather was back in the room, but she could not breathe, could not think. It just did not seem possible: Chik was texting her mom, then only a few hours later she was gone.

With Samantha holding one of Sherokee's limp hands, and Rita holding another, surrounded by loved ones, they all prayed and wished for a miracle, divine intervention, anything to make the little girl's eyes flutter open.

The long, steady beep of a flat line told them hope and prayer would not work this time.

Rita and her daughter continued to hold Sherokee's hands as the little girl's spirit left her body.

No miracles today.

CHAPTER 11

Heather could not be in the same room with her dead child. Samantha was strong because, as she would explain later, she had already lost a son, and Samantha had stayed with him for hours. But Heather could not do it. She stumbled out, and she shared her grief on a Facebook post:

R.I.P. baby girl, I love you sooooooooooo much. Sherokee Rose Harriman, you will definitely be missed.

One by one, the family members left the ICU room, sobbing into tissues, leaning on one another.

As a white sheet was pulled over her lifeless, serene face, 14-year-old Sherokee Rose Harriman was declared deceased at 9:35 p.m.

The coroner completed the examination and made his legal ruling: suicide.

Heather texted Katie Nichols with the news. She knew Katie and Sherokee were close, as close as two girls not blood related could be. Katie was still at the baby shower, celebrating a new life when she received the text:

She's gone

The skinny girl crumpled to the floor sobbing, and everyone at the party now surrounded her with concern. "What's wrong!" "Katie, what's happened?"

All Katie can remember now is how hard she sobbed, over and over, "She's gone! She's gone! She's gone! She's gone!" Until someone scooped her up to hold her close.

Alec Seether's cell phone beeped again, indicating he had another message. He checked the screen and saw it was his friend Katie. Katie were telling him about a text received from Heather. Sherokee was gone. She just passed, Katie texted Alec.

Alec was unsure what that meant. *Passed?*

She gone

Alec could not believe it and they exchanged OMG[3] several times. Katie asked again,

What happened at the park?

Alec typed as fast as his fingertips could hit the screen, his heart pounding so hard he thought he would pass out. His first thought was that he was going to go to jail, although he had no role in Sherokee's death. He was afraid of Sherokee's family blaming him, because they knew him, knew he was present when she stabbed herself. He had no idea what to do, what to say, or what to think with one exception: Alec was convinced he was going to jail.

When she could compose herself enough to text, Katie contacted Angel Hollenbeck. Angel was speechless. Katie could almost see her standing in the middle of the room, clutching her cell phone, staring blankly at nothing. Katie knew that Angel felt guilty, as recent words between herself and Sherokee's had not been friendly.

Angel would feel this way for a long time.

Abraham Ringgold was still pacing the floor, sometimes staring at his cell phone as if willing it to ring. Sherokee

---

3. Oh My God

would be on the other end, he told himself, saying everything was all right. He rarely heard from her anymore and had no idea she were being bullied or teased. Her last words ran over and over in Abe's mind.

"I have a knife." She had said it so bluntly.

"I have a knife." *What happened?*

"I have a—" Abe could not handle the silence. He texted her, wanting to know what happened and if she was okay.

It took a moment, but the reply made him sink to the floor.

The responding text was from Sherokee's mom. Sherokee was dead.

CHAPTER 12

When the hospital bills arrived in the mail, the paperwork made Rita sit down hard, clutching the overwhelming news with shaking hands.

Rita was one of the 1.5 million Tennesseans enrolled in TennCare, the state Medicaid program that provides health insurance to low-income persons, including relatives of dependent children and those on disability. Both Sherokee and Shyloe were on her plan. The final tally for Sherokee's emergency care was for more money than Rita could ever raise, and after her grandchild's demise, she had told others she was grateful TennCare would give her some relief in paying the bill.

But recent court orders, a decrease in federal funding, and a rise in health care costs had forced a large percentage of budget cuts and affected coverage. TennCare did not cover suicide.

Rita called family members. "I'm going to have to declare bankruptcy," she told them.

On Monday, September 6, the day after Sherokee's death, Heather's best friend Abigail Frazier went to Mankin Park just to see where it all took place, to be near where Sherokee last stood. Abigail found the spot where the little girl fell. Abigail was staring at the grass, tears rolling down her face and soaking the front of her blouse, when her thoughts were interrupted by loud laughter from the pavilion area. What she saw there was shocking.

Abigail says she saw Debi Hornsby, Alec Seether, and Donny Duroy all sitting at the picnic tables under the pavilion. They were laughing and talking. "Cutting up, like nothing had even happened there," Abigail says now.

Abigail watched them for a few minutes. Unaware they were being observed, the teens giggled and chattered. They were having a great time, sitting not 500 feet away from where they had watched Sherokee stab herself to death.

SOCIAL MEDIA

@Chikie1295
Sherokee Harriman
Love kids
Love animals
single
straight
7-8 siblings total
live with 1 sibling and feel close to another
lost without a significant other

- Twitter profile of Sherokee Harriman

CHAPTER 13

In February 2004, a few Harvard University roommates gathered to discuss launching a school website. They dubbed it "Facebook." They had no idea it would change communication worldwide, becoming part of society's vernacular. By 2014, it was generating a revenue of over 12 billion dollars, boasting over 1.15 billion active users.

Users register for free, creating their own profile and adding other people as "friends." Users can send messages that can be read in real time or later. They post information to their member page, adding photos and quotes as well as drawings and random thoughts and ideas.

People flocked to Facebook like pilgrims to a cult. They could now connect with lost and new friends. They can keep in touch with family. Members join pages for their alma mater, their hobbies, work, political beliefs, and lifestyles. People can break up, make up, meet, and fight on Facebook.

But one of the problems with the cyber-society is misuse through fake accounts. Anyone can be anybody on Facebook: all it takes is imagination, criminal ideations, or the desire to make a wish come true in cyberspace. Members can take on any persona and "friend" people with the intent of fraud, a process called "cat fishing." A janitor can pretend to be an astronaut, or vice versa. With fake photos and misinformation, a person can look like a movie star. A civilian from Barbados can become a United States military veteran. Criminals can bilk other users out of cash, lurking in cyberspace to stalk.

So while some users are sharing their innermost feelings, others have deceitful intent. It can be shaky ground.

Like millions of people, Sherokee used Facebook as a voice. On June 19, 2015, she shared a video that she had found on Facebook, created with a program called Flipogram. Posting the video to her wall, Sherokee tagged three of her best friends so they would see the video on their own Facebook. She added:

i cried when i got to the middle of the video

The video[4], in scrolling text, read:

Stop bullying - Just imagine this

Your brother/sister Or sibling - comes home from school one day

Tears rolling down their cheeks – You ask them whats Up but you get no reply – You know somethings wrong

You go to them – They are standing in the kitchen – By the knife draw

They tell you whats happend – But its not the first time

Its happened many times before – They tell you That they're worthless

And they have no place Left on earth – And that they want to end it all

You tell them its going to be ok – They go to their room

They write letters – Saying sorry for all the trouble they have caused

But thanking you for being there – They explain whats been happening

For the past few Weeks – They appologise for doing what

---

4. The person who created this video has defunct accounts at this writing and cannot be located, thus cannot be properly cited.

They are about to do – and they love you forever and Always

They pick up the knife – And cut straight down their wrist

They passout – You phone an ambulance – Things are too late

The doctor tells you they did – Everything they Could

But they had lost too much blood – It hits you that you are never

Going to see their face again – Because of the stress of being

Bullied everyday Was just too much – And they felt suicide Was the only option

Its not a nice feeling Is it? – Just remember Words and actions

CAN KILL!!

Dont bully

YouTube was introduced in 2005, and it also literally changed the way people see one another, share and discover new music and information, and voice their opinions. People share, upload, and exchange videos that they created themselves or were created by other individuals or organizations. Kids of today can watch 1950s television commercials. Hopeful singers record themselves, uploading the video in search of a fan base. Many a superstar can thank YouTube for helping to make them international stars.

Sherokee had several YouTube accounts. She posted videos of herself singing, dancing, and lip-synching to her favorite songs, just as millions of other young people do

Just when the world thought it had found the most amazing communication device created since the telephone, along came Twitter in 2006. At this writing, over 100 million users "tweet" (send messages) at the rate of 340 million total per day. Users create a profile (preceded by a @ symbol; one of Sherokee's Twitter accounts was @Chikie1295) and can follow other profiles by adding them to their account. Users group postings between one another by using the hashtag sign (#); for example, #lovemusic, #DallasCowboys, #onetiredmom. Anyone with the same hashtag will see and can use the message. A 2009 study by Pear Analytics revealed 40 percent of tweets are "pointless babble" and only 4 percent is actual news. Nonetheless, Twitter stands as one of the leading communication giants in cyberspace.

And then there is texting/messaging, simply sending messages back and forth, phone to phone, in real time. So cell phones are also a huge part of social media.

Some studies have shown too many people have substituted social media for actual face-to-face social skills, substituting a virtual world for a real one. They have cyber-romances and relationship[s as well as cyber-fights. To "delete" or "add" someone is considered a serious commitment.

With all this technology already in place, Sherokee Harriman was not alone when she posted her feelings on Facebook, tweeted sweet notes about her boyfriends, texted rather than called, and uploaded videos of herself singing. She was a child of a new cyber age, where passing notes in class, using a the home telephone, and even playing music CDs have become archaic notions.

Like everything else, there is a positive and a negative to these inventions. Posting your thoughts, ideas, and woes on Facebook, tweeting and texting them, and uploading videos into cyberspace creates a huge issue: everyone—friend or not—can see what you are feeling and thinking.

Anyone—friend or not—can say what they want from the safety of a phone or keyboard.

Privacy disappears with the click of a button.

The Legacy

I love my mama so much / she is always in my heart
even tho we argue / we will never be apart
she can tell when I have problems /
she knows when I am down
she is always there to cheer me up /
and take away my frowns
at times when I get mad at her / it is hard to stay that way
only because she makes me laugh / every passing day
I love my mother with all my heart /
but this she does not know
sometimes I want to tell her / but I'm afraid to let it show

—poem by Sherokee Harriman, May 30, 2014

CHAPTER 14

Sherokee's maternal grandmother Rita Harriman would later report to psychiatric authorities that she had a great uncle who suffered schizophrenia. But mental illness was not the only problem in her family. Tragedy, alcoholism, and years of abuse would also be regular residents in her home.

Rita Coates and Joseph "Joe" Harriman met on a blind date arranged by one of Joe's relatives. On their first date, Joe brought Rita to one of his relative's homes to babysit. "Don't you have a little son?" he had asked Rita.

"Yes."

"Well, why didn't you bring him?" he asked.

She was taken back. "I didn't think you'd want to watch him, too." It seemed so kind of him.

They married on June 29, 1968, in Illinois. She did not know much about his background. Joe had children from his first marriage, and Rita had children, too. Together they would create a large, blended family that would include children of their own.

Back then, they were listening to the Beatles' *Magical Mystery Tour* album when it hit number one on the charts, a position it would hold for eight weeks. The Harriman household tuned in to "Hollywood Squares" on nighttime television and a new show called "Laugh-In" that was popular for its racy humor. Dr. Martin Luther King had been assassinated at a hotel in Memphis, Tennessee, and recently buried. Thousands of miles away, U.S. Marines raised a flag on a tiny island called Iwo Jima where 7,000 men lost their lives in a ferocious battle.

There were battles under the Harriman roof as well. Both blue-collar workers, Joe was a forklift driver, and Rita worked in a plastics factory. Later in life she would hold degrees in Certified Nurses Aid and Floral Decorating. But now she was just trying to hold life together under the iron fist that ruled her home. "He didn't hit me, but he was verbally abusive," Rita confides. "And he wanted to know where I was going, who I was going with, when I would be back, and where I was all the time." Joe's controlling ways were fueled by copious amounts of alcohol. He was a drunken bully.

Tragedy altered the Harriman's lives on the day 23-year-old Rita was driving her convertible with her two oldest boys, her infant daughter, and a severely mentally challenged cousin also in the car. A faulty tie rod caused the car to crash, sending the boys through the soft roof of the car and causing the cousin to fall onto the baby and into the dashboard.

With no help in sight, Rita walked three miles to a pay phone, having to leave everyone bleeding and bruised in the car. When help arrived, they found the cousin had bit through her lower lip upon impact. The dazed little boys were wandering around in a nearby field. The baby girl was dead from a head injury.

Rita would cry uncontrollably for her lost little girl, but Joe would have none of it. "Stop crying!" he would bark at her. "I don't want to see you cry! Just suck it up! *Shut up!*" He scared her with his shouting and cold-heartedness.

In an attempt to escape Joe's screaming and bullying, Rita quickly learned a survival tactic: never let anyone see tears in her eyes. "I keep it bottled inside," she said.

Joe and Rita raised seven children together. Their sixth child was a girl, Heather, born in early July of 1979 in Kankakee, Illinois, the same town where Rita first came into the world. Heather was raised in Gilman, Illinois, until she was six years old, and the family moved to Smyrna, Tennessee. Heather has called Tennessee "home" ever since, residing in areas in and around LaVergne, Christiana, Murfreesboro, and Woodbury.

Heather grew to mirror her mother with her dark hair, high cheekbones, and small chin; her brown eyes always seemed stormy. As Heather grew, Rita sensed a restless spirit in her dark-eyed daughter. "She was rebellious," Rita explains. "She just always seemed like she wanted people to like her. But she was so angry." She wonders if it was because, when Heather tried something new, she was often outshone. Heather joined ROTC in school and enjoyed it. Then another sibling also joined ROTC and excelled in it, became quite involved, and even got to attend the ROTC Ball, a formal affair.

"Heather didn't get to go," Rita says. "She was grounded for not doing what she was told."

Joe's abusive words only escalated the stormy relationships in the home. The alcohol made the children hate and fear him; at the same time, they loved him because he was their father. But the hate simmered in Heather, though she tried to push it away and, like her mother, "tough it out."

"We were raised tough," one of Heather's sisters says now. Their father was never one to show emotion, and their mother's feelings seemed to be locked behind heavy, dark doors. Several of her children recall their mother beating them across the back with shoes and hands for their indiscretions. Rita's anger seemed to unleash itself when administering discipline. All of those pent-up emotions had to go somewhere, recalls one of her children. Meanwhile, Joe continued to guzzle alcohol and treat his wife and kids like objects that he owned. If Rita was talking on the telephone he would demand, "Who are you talking to? Why are you on the phone for so long? What were you yapping about now?"

One of his daughters did not dodge fast enough, and he hit her over the head with a beer bottle. Another girl bore the brunt of his beatings, wondering why she was the only daughter who would end up nursing bruises. The boys dodged fists and kicks. Yet they all craved love and positive attention from their father.

Heather sums up her childhood: "My life was hell."

CHAPTER 15

"You have to be tough and stand up," Joe advised his children about schoolyard bullies. "Stand your ground and don't walk away!"

But when Joseph Harriman bullied his kids, they dared not stand up to him. Standing their ground meant a beating, mental abuse, and filthy name-calling. His children learned quickly never to question, to do as they were told, never cry, and obey his word. The best thing to do was just to avoid home.

Heather was eight and her sisters were not much older when their father called them in to stand in a straight line before him. He pointed at Heather. "Ya'll are nothing but a bunch of bitches"—the finger wavered and pointed to the next daughter—"whores"—and to the third child—"and sluts." They dared not respond.

Joe was mean, but he was a meaner drunk. "Drunk or sober, he treated mom like crap," Heather recalls. "She would cower down in a corner, shaking" from fear.

One of Joe's sons can remember being beat down, then physically thrown out the front door to land on the pavement, then bullied and beaten more with the other brothers. Another sibling echoes the recollection.

"I always thought Joe was jealous of the boys," Rita reflects back. "Why, I don't know." She does not remember him being physically abusive with their daughters.

Money was always tight, which meant necessities were always more important than luxuries; a blue-collar salary for a large family meant no new clothes, flashy jewelry, or a car. While other kids could talk and giggle about the new movie theater while driving around town, or about going to the mall, the Harriman kids could only watch and listen, pretending they did not care.

Heather remained miserable at home. Then there were the kids at school who provided constant harassment and bullying. The names followed her everywhere Heather went; it just felt like a safe place was nonexistent.

"Here comes fatso!"

"Where'd you get your dress—Salvation Army?"

"What are you, stupid? Hey—stupid girl!"

At home or at school, she was too fat, too poor, too stupid, and ugly. It never ended.

This bullying and the world around her escalated to the point that a fourteen-year-old Heather found herself sitting alone in the Harriman home, feeling scared, alone, and hopeless. "My life sucks," she told herself over and over. "My life sucks." She could never please her father, she was afraid of her mother, and she would never find anyone who truly loved her. So she took care of it the best way she knew how.

Heather calmly walked to the bathroom, poured a handful of pills into a shaking palm, and began downing them. It was time to just end it all, and 175 pills at 500 milligrams each should do it.

Instead, she endured the pain of having her stomach pumped in the emergency room, then was placed on suicide watch for three days. When she arrived home, her parents babied her and made sure she was happy and feeling safe, surrounding her with the love she craved. On the fourth day, "It was back to normal," Heather recalls, with the same beatings and the name-calling and bullying. "It's like they didn't learn the lesson of being nice."

There had to be something she could escape. She dropped out of high school to escape the taunts and the feelings of being stupid, but would spend a lifetime regretting that decision.

Meanwhile, life at home remained a battleground.

Leaving Joe was not an option for Rita. This was not a time where women left abusive men. She would not be able to take care of her kids on her meager salary and limited education. "You stayed married no matter what," Heather says now. "Back then you just stuck it out." The first battered women's shelter for American women did not open until the early 1970s. It would take 16 years before Domestic Violence Awareness Month would be held in the United States. It would take Heather Harriman many more years to understand it all.

Finally, after eight years of his drinking, Rita summoned up the courage to give Joe an ultimatum. "It's either the kids or the booze," she told him. "If you want to keep drinking that's fine, but I'm leaving and taking the kids with me."

Joe sobered up, but was still abusive. "You fat whores!" he raged at his daughters, even without the help of alcohol. "Sluts!"

This was the family legacy Sherokee Harriman would inherit.

CHAPTER 16

Heather Harriman was racing through the housing projects where she lived, Abigail Frazier at her side. They were 15 and 13, respectfully, and best friends, so it wasn't unusual to see the two girls together and running from trouble.

Heather stopped to catch her breath just in front of the apartment where she lived with her parents and siblings. Abigail crashed into her, and both girls shrieked with merriment.

Heather spent as much time with Abigail as possible. "I was wild," Heather admits honestly. Yet despite all of the pain Joe caused, "I was still seeking my dad's approval."

"We were wild kids," Abigail giggles now. "And always together. If you saw one of us, then you saw the other."

Abigail lived with her single mom and multiple siblings. Even at her very young age, it was Abigail's responsibility to make dinners, ensure that homework was done, keep the house tidy, and get everyone off to school. Her mother worked two jobs to keep her family fed, clothed, and taken care of. Abigail's mother had been a teenaged unwed mother, and now she worked hard to keep their family together. It also left Abigail unsupervised, and most of her time was spent with Heather. Theirs was a kinship not unlike sisterhood.

Abigail did not think badly of or disrespect her friend just because Heather's family had little money. She knew that both of Heather's parents were now on disability; her father suffered from COPD and was always sickly. Abigail also knew his constant illness and breathing issues did not keep him from being abusive, and he was not one to mince words, particularly with his children. Abigail will explain how Heather's mother, Rita, "was never as intense" as her husband, but Rita was powerless to stop his cursing at their children. When one of his teenaged daughters announced her unplanned pregnancy, Abigail remembers Joe snapping at the cowering girl. "Well, this wouldn't have happened if you weren't spreading your legs, being a slut."

As a recovering alcoholic, the one thing Joe forbade in his home was drinking. "He'd make you sleep on the porch before he would let you come in the house if you had been drinking," Abigail remembers. Even at a young age, Abigail saw how each of the Harriman clan handled their angst in various ways: Heather decided drinking and smoking pot was her best escape. When she was high and drunk, there were no problems in the blurry haze. For once, Heather could relax, clear of pain, sadness, and fear. But Heather's true addiction did not reside in a bottle or in a pill: it was to the male species that she could rarely say "no."

Heather liked having a boy around, a male who liked *her*. It made her feel wanted, needed, and she was *someone*. Abigail and their tight-knit group of friends counted Heather as a loyal buddy "until there was a man around," says a close friend. "It was her self esteem. She just didn't seem sure of herself, so she had to have a man to 'love' her. To take care of her."

Heather was always seeking the perfect relationship, confusing sex with love. After she dropped out of school, she began a flotsam existence based on a need for love and attention. "The first time I had sex, I thought I was pregnant. I had to tell my parents," she remembered. Feeling so alone, nauseated with fear and worry, she finally confided in them.

She recalls that Rita responded, "You're a whore."

Joe followed with, "You're a slut."

Heather was relieved when her period started. She was not pregnant, after all. But the happiness was short-lived.

Happiness at her house was always short-lived.

Heather left home as soon as she could find an escape route. Her boyfriend Ronnie was that route. She was living with three other friends, including Ronnie, when she took the pregnancy test that showed positive. They were elated because they wanted a baby. Heather and Ronnie felt they were ready for parenthood. Maybe a child would take away some of life's bleakness.

Heather and Ronnie moved into an apartment with one of Heather's girlhood friends. Eventually, the friend had to move out of the apartment, leaving it to Heather.

Heather loved Ronnie and hoped they could settle down and be a little family. She was convinced he was *the one*. So desperate for the family bonding she never had, she made herself overlook his criminal record and his addictions. He *had* to be "the one." They were going to have a baby.

Shyloe Noel was born in July 1999. Shyloe was a pretty little girl, with flaxen hair and a big smile. They called her "Shy."

But there was something wrong with Shy: her attention span seemed nonexistent. She did not develop as quickly as other babies and demanded twice the care.

Heather curbed the partying and the late nights for a while. Still, she would later confide, "I wish someone would have come along to drag me out by my hair and beat the shit out of me, because I wasn't a good mom."

SHEROKEE

I'm feeling loved and unloved

—Sherokee Harriman on her Facebook
timeline, July 7, 2013

"That baby has had problems since
she came into this world."

—Family friend

CHAPTER 17

When Mack Edwards accepted an invitation to go to an amusement park called Six Flags, he had no idea his life was about to change... and change him forever.

It began simply enough. Mack's uncle invited him and a few friends and family members to the theme park. Mack's cousin went along and brought a friend named Heather Harriman. Heather was pretty, sporting long, thick, dark hair; big brown eyes; and a dry wit. Mack was short, just a bit taller than her: they fit together. Mack liked her, and they spent the day riding the amusement park rides, sipping drinks, eating fast food, and laughing and talking. Soon Mack asked for her phone number, and a romance began. Ronnie went to the wayside.

But trouble got in the way, despite their attraction. Mack, a self-admitted alcoholic, explains now, "I was young. I didn't want to settle down. I wanted to run around with my friends; I was wild."

Mack recalls that Heather could not accept his drinking and drug use. Alcohol fueled an anger in Mack: he became an intimidating and scary bully. A typical addict, Mack selected drugs and alcohol over relationships, and it caused the break-up. Heather left him.

Mack returned to his hometown of Mansfield, Ohio. He was raised in this town since he first opened his eyes to the world in December 1981. He continued to be a hell-raiser, a bad boy, but he never forgot the dark-haired girl he left in Nashville.

He eventually moved back to Tennessee, and his move involved contacting Heather. They talked and tried dating again, hoping it would work out. She still found Mack handsome in a rugged way, with his intense blue eyes, dark hair, and chin whiskers.

Heather was living in an apartment with Mack Edwards and a few friends when a pregnancy test confirmed she was going to have another baby.

Mack was a fully dependent addict, and alcohol continued to fuel a restless anger inside of him. Heather became afraid of Mack when he drank, and because he drank often, the relationship ended yet again. Mack did not want to stop drinking, and Heather wanted someone to love her and take care of her. They tried to make it work, but it was over. He was still young and wanted to party, but Heather was not about to let her heart be broken again.

CHAPTER 18

Heather gave birth to her second child on November 7, 2000.

When she went into labor, Heather was living at her parent's home and chafing at the bit to escape. Heather was rushed to the hospital and preparing to give birth when tests revealed the fetus was experiencing stress, and Heather was suffering from birth-related complications. Heather was forced to have a C-section to deliver at 10:08 p.m., and her little girl had to be taken away for treatment immediately. Heather was not allowed to hold her until 4 a.m. The newborn spent her first few days in an incubator to keep her alive. "I was closer to her," Heather admits, "because she almost died and I almost died." An immediate bond seemed to grow between them as a result.

"Heather did not bond with Shy, because Shy was so hard to take care of. She had so many problems," one of Heather's siblings confided. "But when Sherokee came along! Heather was crazy about Sherokee. She thought Sherokee was the greatest thing ever."

She named her daughter Sherokee Rose. Heather pronounced it "Cherokee," like the Native American tribe. Sherokee was dubbed "Chik."

The Cherokee Rose is the state flower of Georgia. Legend has it that during the Trail of Tears, when thousands of Native Americans were force-marched across the United States, the Cherokee mothers cried mightily because they were unable to assist children in surviving the journey. The elders lifted prayers to their gods for a sign that would give these mothers strength. Cherokee Roses sprouted where the tears had fallen to the earth. The flowers are white for tears; the golden center represents the riches stolen from the Cherokee tribes, and the seven petals represent the seven Cherokee clans. The flower grows wild in certain locations where so many marched… and many died.

More tears were to flow, both happy and sad, during Sherokee's early life. It seems like she came into world already surrounded by chaos.

Baby Sherokee did not get to leave the hospital until the day after Heather was home from the hospital. The baby continued to experience health problems once she was home. Her health was closely monitored the first few months of her life, and she had to be on a machine to help her breathe. Sherokee stopped breathing at least once during feeding and had to wear a heart monitor. She had to be bundled up in her crib, and Heather would play Mozart recordings in the room to help the baby relax. The cold-natured little girl would insist on wearing long sleeved shirts into her toddler years. Sherokee would suffer susceptibility to cold germs the rest of her life.

Shy and Sherokee had been born with so many problems, Rita wonders today if their poor health was caused by Heather's smoking cigarettes. Rita asks herself if Heather had been using drugs or if the girls' fathers' were using.

Still, Sherokee was a sunny baby with chubby cheeks, still chubby as she began toddling, then walking. "You're my little chunky monkey!" an aunt would tease, swooping up the little girl for kisses. Sherokee would gurgle with joy and always return kisses and hugs. She was so sweet and full of giggles. She laughed and smiled, truly enjoying the world around her.

The little sisters got along initially. Sherokee would point at Shyloe and talk to her in gurgles and baby talk when they were toddlers. She made the family laugh one day when she was fussing at her "Sissy" in baby talk, shaking a stern finger at Shyloe as she jabbered.

Unfortunately, motherhood did not settle Heather. Heather's work record remained as sporadic as her addresses. She worked for a time at the collections drop-off at Goodwill Industries. Then there was a warehouse job, and employment at different times at various gas stations. Still regretting not having a high school diploma, she did start GED classes, but never completed them. Heather just always seemed to be searching, to be needing. Her self esteem was nonexistent. "She has been in a slump for so long, it seems she's just accepted it," reports a close friend. "I don't think it's clinical depression. I just think she wants to be loved. She wants to be needed. And she hates to be alone."

Another friend adds, "It's almost like she had no want or drive. She has nothing, and she's content with having nothing. And she just wants a man to take care of her, to love her."

Heather agrees with both sentiments, and she admits she learned the hard way how women who are trying so hard to find the perfect mate can be open targets for abusers. Heather confirms, "I was looking for something serious, but I always seemed to find the wrong ones."

When Jamie Duke met Heather, he found someone he could bully with verbal abuse, and he began releasing his anger on her. This was exactly what he had done to his ex-wife, Amy Duke.

"*Nobody* liked Jamie," Amy says flatly. But the Jamie–Heather relationship did render one good result: Amy met Heather, who became a "sister" to her. "Heather is a ball of energy! I just love her," Amy says. "She just loves everyone, no matter what." This included Amy and Jamie's children, who resided with Amy. Heather would accompany Jamie on his visitation days when he went to see his children at Amy's home, and she brought Shyloe and Sherokee to play with the Duke children. Heather enjoyed spending time with the kids.

"But I don't want to cross any boundaries," she told Amy, who assured her she was happy Jamie had found a woman so wonderful. Heather was great with the Duke children and was respectful of Amy and Jamie's former marriage.

Still, she was seeking. Heather would get a job, then leave it. She moved around the LaVergne area, with this friend here or that group there, and with her family only as a last resort. She was still "the black sheep" in a family of seven siblings. Her brothers and sisters, says a family member, "did well for themselves, and the oldest boy has always been a self-made man." Heather just seemed to be searching.

She thought she had found happiness when she met Nate.

"It was a whirlwind romance that ended up in hell," Heather says bluntly of her marriage to Nate Rodriguez. They both thought they were in love; they both believed they found the perfect soul mate. In 2001, Heather and Nate Rodriguez said, "I do," in a simple wedding. Finally, she had found someone who loved her, who treated her right. He was convinced she was the answer to what he was looking for. But in just a few years, they would separate and she would file for divorce. She never looked back.

Heather's best friend Abigail became an unmarried mother at a young age; the responsibility forced her, she said, to "grow up, and take care of my child." She wanted a future, financial security, which meant escaping the hand-to-mouth existence she was living. She hoped Heather would follow her example.

Now that she was a parent, Heather's family also hoped she would settle down and be a good mother. Maybe now she would calm down.

These hopes were quickly dashed. She was back with Shyloe's father, Ronnie, trying to make it work. Theirs was a meager existence; the apartment had to be heated with space heaters. There were no faucets on the tub: instead, they used a wrench to twist the extending pipe so water would gush out of the spigot. Their place never seemed clean, so matter how often they would scrub.

Still, they had each another. At least being with someone would help tolerate the living conditions. It could always be worse...

The bus driver smiled at the cute but somber five-year-old girl who climbed the steps into the bus that was taking her to kindergarten. The little girl was wearing the same clothes she had worn yesterday when the bus picked her up, which was the same outfit she had worn the day prior to that one. The bus driver's nose wrinkled as Shyloe walked past. Shyloe smelled of urine.

Per law, the bus driver made a note; a phone call was placed to the Department of Human Services (DHS). When DHS finally became involved, Shyloe's physical state was not the sole focus of their investigation.

This time, Heather and Ronnie's relationship had lasted about a month. Some family and friends felt Heather turned Shyloe and Sherokee's care over to Ronnie so she would have more freedom. A friend of Ronnie's reports that Ronnie fed, bathed, dressed, and took care of Shyloe and Sherokee. He appeared to be the doting father. Regardless of the truth, Ronnie's involvement was about to become the catalyst for a life-long fall.

It all erupted one night in 2004 when one of Heather's friends picked up her phone and heard Heather's voice on the other end. The story she told made the friend drop into a chair, grasping the phone.

CHAPTER 19

Shyloe made the first outcry. "Ronnie touched me, and he makes me touch him." She then described the sexual abuse she suffered at her father's hand.

Sherokee had told Heather, "It hurts," and would indicate her vaginal area. Then she said, "Ronnie touched me and made it hurt down there!"

Heather's friend raced to the apartment to pack up Heather, Sherokee, and Shyloe. What she saw when she walked in the door was horrifying.

According to several witnesses, Shyloe was filthy. Her hair was unwashed. She did not appear to have been bathed or taken care of. Sherokee's physical condition was not much better.[5] Repulsed, the friend drove Heather and the babies to the nearest emergency room[6]. Friends and family recall it was Christmas Day.

Rita was sitting in church during worship on December 26 when her cell phone rang, and the caller broke the horrific news. Rita dug through her purse, but she did not have gas money. The congregation pooled some money and gave her the cash to put gas in her van so she could get to the hospital. In minutes, she was heading for a hospital in Smyrna, a town

---

5. Heather denies the state of the girl's physical appearances, declaring the reports as exaggerations. The DHS records have been sealed.

6. Neither friends or family can recall the name of the hospital. Records at one Shelbyville hospital have been destroyed.

of just over 43,000 which shares a border with LaVergne. When she arrived, she learned the worst.

Shyloe was telling the authorities about Ronnie molesting her. Social service workers were also questioning Sherokee, who now was refusing to admit that Ronnie hurt her.

A few relatives recall both girls were unwashed, a mess, to the point of smelling horrible. Dried urine stained their clothing, which had not been changed in days. They did not have shoes on. Their hair was tangled and had not been combed in a while. Both girls had rashes in their pubic area and a yeast infection from Ronnie.

Heather's sister Samantha arrived at the hospital and was directed to a room where a police officer, a nurse, and a doctor were with the girls. She says when she walked in she was hit with the stench of urine. Both girls, sobbing and screaming, clung to her, their little faces red and swollen from crying. Their screams echoed off the hospital room walls. It seemed the tears just would not stop. Samantha's shoulders were drenched as the tears ran down. She squeezed them tight, her lips moving in silent prayer. She thought they would never let go. "It's all right," she told them over and over, her own tears flowing down her cheeks. "You're safe." She held on, even as her nostrils were assaulted with the stench of urine and filth. DHS opened a file. The little girls spent a night in foster care once they were released from the hospital.

A DHS representative would later contact Rita and ask her to meet. It was during this meeting when Rita learned Shyloe had been missing a lot of school; Shelbyville School had a long list of her absences. Heather and another family member were also at the meeting.

"There was a complaint from Shyloe's bus driver," the DHS worker explained, rifling through pages. "Shyloe had worn the same clothes for three days and smelled like urine."

The DHS employee interviewed Heather, who admitted to a history of smoking marijuana and drinking. She remained a chain smoker, but did not currently "use drugs." A plan was put in place for the future of the family: Heather was to attend parenting classes and addiction counseling. Then, after she graduated from the classes, they would meet in court to determine if she could have custody of the girls.

"Until then, the girls will either remain in state custody, or their grandparents can keep them."

State custody sounded ominous and cold. It was also frightening: enough kids had been abused in foster care, Rita knew. And Shyloe and Sherokee were blood kin.

Heather was furious and hurt. It seemed she could do nothing right. She was a horrible child, a terrible person, and now an ogre of a mother. "Why are you pushing my buttons!" she raged at her mother. "Why are you trying to make me so angry!" she swore at the DHS official and cursed loudly about the situation.

"Stop it, Heather!" Rita ordered. "You're not hurting anyone but yourself."

"I don't give a fuck!" Heather raged at Rita. "Fuck this bullshit! You just see dollar signs because of the money you'll be getting!" She slumped back in her seat. "You bitches are making me truly, extremely, extremely upset! You're pushing my fucking buttons on purpose!"

The social worker continued to scribble notes. An anger management class was added to Heather's required itinerary.

Years later Heather would admit, embarrassed, "I blew up like an idiot."

CHAPTER 20

Joe and Rita owned a house on a nice residential block in Shelbyville. They could provide a home where each girl would have her own room. DHS approved the babies staying with their maternal grandparents until a court date. Heather was to sign up for the required classes. DHS performed home checks every six months to ensure the girls were clean, eating properly, attending school, seeing a counselor, and had their own rooms as promised. A counselor from ABC Behavior in Lebanon, Tennessee, performed home visits with Sherokee and Shyloe.

It all sounded wonderful, but Heather's siblings were aghast. "What the hell," they asked one another, "is DHS thinking?" Joe and Rita were in their 50s, having raised a household of children who grew up dodging angry words and angry hands, bullied their whole lives. Was DHS aware of that abuse?

Heather had no job, no high school diploma or GED, and did not drive nor own a vehicle. She was not in a relationship. She felt like a failure as a parent. She feared but loved her parents in such a confusing way. Shyloe had a learning disorder. Sherokee was already troubled at only a few years old. Heather's life continued to spiral out of control, and she had never felt so lost at what to do or where to go. A good friend sat her down and gave trusted advice. "The best thing you can do right now," Heather was told, "is to let your parents adopt those girls and get your shit together."

"The girls have what they deserve," Heather agreed. "I can't provide any of that." She had to do the right thing now.

Heather and her siblings still remained confused over their relationships with their parents. Like thousands of dysfunctional families in the country, they loved one another as fiercely as they despised each other. As in so many abusive homes, the children wanted to run away from their parents as much as they needed to run into the arms of the same people who abused them. Everyone was just trying to survive, day by day, using what little they knew as a compass.

DNA tests were completed on the girls as part of the custody case. At least two paternity tests were performed to rule out two possible men as Sherokee's biological father. "Then the only person it could be," Heather told friends, "is Mack." But by then, Mack was long gone out of her life. "He wouldn't care," Heather told friends. "He wouldn't give a shit about this little girl, so I'm sure as hell not telling him. She doesn't need that in her life."

Shyloe's father Ronnie fled to a halfway house where, the Harrimans explain, authorities could not arrest him. Eventually he slipped out of the halfway house into the streets and off the radar. He never saw the inside of a jail cell for abusing Shyloe and Sherokee because he simply disappeared.

Once they were away from Ronnie and the apartment, the girls began to take great pride in having their space. "My room!" Shyloe would tell visitors, her little fingers winding around the adult's hand and leading them to see her room. "Sissy's room!" She would lead them to Sherokee's little bedroom.

Heather was scheduled to take a state-run parenting course and a drug and alcohol class. She would later say she was not given the proper information so was unable to attend the classes. She told a friend she did not drive so she could never attend. So her girls continued living with their maternal grandparents.

Joe and Rita discussed legally adopting their grandchildren. "I don't want to do this," Joe told Rita. "We've raised kids. This is *our* time."

Rita disagreed. They were flesh and blood. "I don't want them going to the state," she insisted. It was one of the rare times she won an argument.

The Harrimans went to court. Official papers were eventually filed, and Shyloe and Sherokee were legally adopted by Heather's parents in September 2006.

Heather recalls, "I had to grow up and realize I shouldn't have done this. Getting them taken away from me was a real eye-opener." Shyloe and Sherokee became legal wards of the home that Heather had so desperately wanted to escape.

Sherokee and Shyloe called Rita "Gran," never their "Mom." Joe was "Grandpa." Neither Rita nor Joe demanded the girls call them their parents. The girls were aware of who "mom" was, they knew "mom" was just not able to be with them right now.

Despite his initial arguments, Joe Harriman fell in love with his granddaughters and treated them with kindness. His favorite child was Sherokee, and he would get angry when Rita tried to correct the little girl with the white-blonde hair. "Don't be so hard on her," he would chastise Rita when she tried to discipline her. "Sherokee is Paw-paw's girl!" Joe would scoop her up and tickle her, hugging her close. With Shyloe it was a different story. Rita tended to baby her because of her learning disabilities. "Stop treating her different!" Joe's voice would boom. "Treat her normal, so she don't grow up feeling bad about herself!"

Shy became "Gran's girl."

Rita recalls Joe was not abusive with the little girls; he never treated them as he had his own children. He was patient and kind. He was an entirely different man.

Then his health began to deteriorate. His mind slogging through the hazy fog of dementia, Joseph Harriman became physically abusive to Rita. Like a child, he would strike out at her when he did not get his way, arguing and swinging a fist. He was the epitome of the schoolyard bully: angry, obstinate, and scaring those less powerful than him, which was everyone in the house. Just because he was now restricted to a wheelchair did not mean he was any less frightening.

"Mom still caters to him," her children complained to one another. Rita rushed away from the hospital bedside of one teenaged daughter, who was holding her own newborn child, "because it was time to fix Daddy his supper." In the new mother's eyes, Rita left a terrified teenager alone in a hospital bed so Joe could be served a meal at a certain time.

It seemed to many family members that Shy and Chik went from one dysfunctional home life into another.

Sherokee initially saw a doctor at ABC Behavioral in Lebanon. She would later be a patient at the Guidance Center. The child would be prescribed Geodon, but it had no effect. The medical personnel also tried Tenex, Vyvanse, and Depakote. Each medication would work for a time, then lose its effect, and Sherokee was angry and unhappy again.

The pretty little blonde girl's smiles had been replaced with scowls and tears. She rarely laughed now.

Samantha sadly recalled, "Sherokee had been a happy little kid. She loved kisses and hugs, she laughed and played. [The molestation] broke her spirit. It just broke her spirit."

CHAPTER 21

Sherokee and Shyloe would receive counseling for the abuse they suffered. But Ronnie had escaped prosecution, and the girl's lives were uprooted; their mother could not take care of them and their grandparents struggled with finances and their own welfare. Although they did have fun at times, anger was always brewing.

As a kindergartener, Shyloe went to counseling at Smyrna Guidance Center and was diagnosed with ADHD and Asperger's Syndrome. She was also identified as mildly mentally challenged.

Before she entered kindergarten, Sherokee was diagnosed as bipolar with Attention Deficit Hyperactivity Disorder (ADHD). She was also suffering from Post Traumatic Stress Disorder (PTSD) and anger issues.

The *Diagnostic and Statistical Manual of Mental Disorders* (*DSM*), published by the American Psychiatric Association, uses a multitude of resources to standardize and define psychiatric diagnostic criteria and categories. While it has its naysayers, the DSM continues to be the resource for the mental health field, the legal system, pharmaceutical companies, and clinicians. As defined by the *DSM*, bipolar disorder is a "mood disorder" in which a person's mood is the underlying feature in abnormal behavior. It is characterized as an incident of at least one manic or mixed-manic episode in a lifetime. The disorder is cyclic: the person cycles into mania, then back around to their normal state, then into a downfall of depression. It was once labeled manic-depressive illness.

The manic symptoms include thoughts that leap from one topic to another, resulting in scattered thinking. Bipolars report increased energy, concentration problems, and trouble sleeping during the manic episodes. Their actions may also be scattered, and decisions are made with little thought of consequences. It is as they are racing through life with no time for consideration or preparation, pell-mell toward a cliff, then they fall off the ledge into the void of depression. In this stage, they will sleep often and for prolonged periods, yet insist they are exhausted. It is true depression: loss of interest in life, social activity, work, and hobbies that once held passion. There is loss of energy and withdrawal from people, as well as a decline in their appearance and self care.

There are degrees of bipolar disorder. A mixed-manic episode contains elements of both manic and depressive episodes; it is not as common but does last longer. The mood disorder swings even more severely, from crying and feeling hopeless to being chatty and the "life of the party."

The Mayo Clinic reports there is no known cause of bipolar disorder. It may be caused by an imbalance of neurotransmitters. Environmental factors may play a role; a life event can trigger a mood episode in the predisposition for bipolar disorder. The cause may be genetic. What is known is that bipolar disorder is a biological disorder occurring in the brain.

Medication for stabilization, together with behavior therapy, can help. Medication must be carefully monitored by a physician, and every medication has varying side effects. In addition, medications must be adjusted and changed over time as the body becomes immune to the chemicals released into the system.

Sherokee was prescribed Abilify for some time until she was placed on Latuda, which unfortunately has side effects that include weight gain, drowsiness, akathisia (a movement disorder characterized by a feeling of inner restlessness and a compelling need to be in constant motion), or nausea. Medication affects people in different ways, though; while some patients on Latuda report weight gain, Sherokee felt it curbed her appetite.

Anti-depressants must be monitored carefully: studies have shown they can increase the risk of suicidal thoughts in some children, teens, and young adults.[7]

Bipolar disorder, like so many other disorders, can be misdiagnosed. For some time, professionals agree, it was the "diagnosis of the month," meaning it was an overused label often slapped on a misdiagnosed patient.

Sherokee may not have known she shared the same disorder many famous and talented individuals had or have. It is probable that Ludwig Von Beethoven was bipolar. Vincent Van Gogh, Abraham Lincoln, and Mark Twain displayed the symptoms. Actors Burgess Meredith, Vivien Leigh, and Carrie Fisher were diagnosed bipolar, along with astronaut Buzz Aldrin and political leader Winston Churchill. So a mood disorder is not a prerequisite for failure. Some historians and sociologists believe talented, famous, and powerful people would not have enjoyed such success had they not had a mood disorder that places thinking and reasoning on a different plane, enhancing creativity: such people think outside the norm, utilizing reasoning that other people find difficult to comprehend.

Unless someone understands bipolar disorder, he or she may label it with a different name: crazy.

The National Institute of Mental Health defines post traumatic stress disorder (PTSD) as "a disorder that develops in some people who have seen or lived through a shocking, scary, or dangerous event." Where once it was associated with military veterans who experienced the traumatic

---

7. "Side Effects of Latuda" Latuda medication warning labels and medication profile

experience of war, multiple studies have confirmed PTSD occurs in many incidents: surviving a horrific incident, abuse from a significant other, witnessing a disaster, and surviving a traumatic period of time, including child abuse.

Fear triggers reaction in the physical body. People with PTSD will feel frightened or stressed even when safe. The stress is caused by a "trigger," an incident that brings back all of those old feelings, emotions, physical changes, and psychological reactions. For example, a war veteran may feel instant fear when hearing the rotor blades of a helicopter as it flies benignly over his home. The veteran's symptoms are constant, but hearing the helicopter is the trigger causing physical and psychological reactions, which might include feeling tense or anxious and having angry outbursts.

Symptoms of PTSD include negative thoughts about oneself or the world, distorted feelings like guilt or blame, and loss of interest in enjoyable activities.

The National Institute of Mental Health reports that children younger than six years old who are experiencing PTSD may wet the bed (after toilet training), forget how to talk or be unable to talk, act out the scary event during playtime, and be unusually clingy with a parent or other adult. "Older children and teens are more likely to show symptoms similar to those seen in adults. They may also develop disruptive, disrespectful, or destructive behaviors. They may also have thoughts of revenge."[8]

Triggers. Negative thoughts about oneself and their world. Disruptive behavior. Thoughts of revenge. All would be a part of Sherokee Harriman's life as she grew.

At such a young age, Sherokee had to deal with the imbalances in her brain that made her so depressed she could not function, then so manic she could not control her urges or behaviors; her words and actions ran the gamut from

8. The National Institute of Mental Health (NIMH) publication "Post Traumatic Stress Disorder in Children." NIH Publication No. TR-08-6388

socially unacceptable to frightening to funny. Often she told everyone who was within range of her voice, "I hate you!" and "Nobody loves me!" She began threatening suicide at age three.

"Sherokee has been on medication forever," confides a family friend.

Samantha recalls, "The medicine just seemed to make her angry. I don't think any of it helped." The little girl with the beautiful smile was a bed wetter, refused to shower or keep clean, and was violent. "She would go to school and the kids would really bully her then, saying she stunk," a family member recalls.

And then there was the family dog Sherokee killed. She fell onto the little dog, and it yelped in pain. The family rushed it to the vet but nothing could be done; the little pup suffered a broken back.

She later admitted she did it on purpose. When the dog was euthanized, a family member says, "Sherokee laughed about it."

Sherokee was admitted into kindergarten at Smyrna Elementary in August of 2006 when she was five years old. She was now a part of the Rutherford County School System, an organization her family would come to loathe. School records show she was absent only two days in the school year and never tardy. There were four parent conferences held that school year.

Sherokee brought home her report card at the end of the year, and her family read the S (satisfactory) grades for communication skills and general classes; she made S+ in math and in reading.

But not all was well. Kindergartener Sherokee came marching into the house one day after school. Another little student had angered her. She complained to her family, "That little girl is a bitch, and I don't want to play with her anymore."

Family members thought it was hysterical, a child using the term "bitch."

She was passed to first grade.

CHAPTER 22

Initially, Heather was only allowed to talk to her children on the telephone. Then she was allowed supervised visits. Eventually, the visits were extended. Sometime in 2007 or 2008, she was able to visit, unsupervised, with her daughters. Heather tried desperately to make up for the time she was away from the girls, still bouncing in and out of their lives because of the rules set forth by DHS. She was consumed with guilt for becoming the type of mother she swore she would never be, yet she was still desperately trying to find solace in male companionship. Never having received any sort of training or counseling, and without positive parenting role models, Heather did what she thought was right at the time.

As she made her way through elementary school, little Sherokee was sent to doctors who suggested psychiatrists and psychologists, who tried medication and therapy. "That baby," a family friend confides, "has had problems since she came into this world."

Sherokee hated school as she entered her first-grade classroom at Smyrna Elementary in 2007. While she was "slow to turn in work," according to her report card, her grades showed "S" in all classes except math, language, and spelling, where an S+ appeared on her report card. She was reading at grade level. Eight months into the first grade, students were given a standardized test to determine their mastery in core subjects. While her grades in social studies and science were not as good as math and languages, her grades were at the same levels of the national percentile of students taking the tests.

She missed three days of school that first year. She was passed into second grade.

The note from school officials landed in Heather's lap in November 2008 while Sherokee was attending Smyrna Elementary as a second grader. It was a "warning notice" that little Sherokee was a thief: she was stealing pencils, pens, gum, candy, and money belonging to students and even a teacher. If it continued, school officials warned Heather, then Sherokee would be suspended.

When an intervention with her teacher did not solve the problem, there was a counseling session in the school guidance office with the assistant principal sitting in. Despite the work with school officials, the stealing continued.

Heather recalls, "The school called me up one time, asking me if I was missing any money. Somehow Sherokee had $10 or $20 dollars on her." The phone call was logged as a telephonic parental conference.

On an undated Student Information Profile, "Independent Work Skills" reveals Sherokee worked well with others. There is also a note under Behavior: *stealing*.

In January 2009 the notice came:

Sherokee has habitually stole items at school this year. A letter went home in November about this behavior stating an out-of-school suspension would be the next intervention.

Second-grader Sherokee was suspended for one day on January 23, 2009.

Her reading and math scores show "at grade level" with one report; her math skills dipped on a separate report. Sherokee could do work, but her analytical and problem-solving skills were lacking. Where once she did well in reading, now her reading comprehension began showing problems. Yet the final grade report card shows grades ranging from one "I" (improving) to "E" (excellent).

She was passed into third grade. She still hated school. A pattern was set for the rest of her life.

CHAPTER 23

There was a new perceived torment in Sherokee's life called the Tennessee Comprehensive Assessment Program (TCAP). This standardized testing program is issued to all students in Tennessee public schools, beginning in the third grade. TCAP shows what the child has learned in the past school year and acts as a guide to prepare the child for the next year of education. Students are tested in reading, language arts, social studies, mathematics, and science.

Reading TCAP results is difficult. Initially, the reader sees a series of lines, tiny black diamonds, and various circles. There are several detailed pages listing student results. It takes careful reading and studying for the layman to understand the nature of the test and how it is scored.

Third-grader Sherokee took the TCAP in March 2008 to measure what she had learned during her first two years in school. Her testing scores showed "Mastery" in both communication (reading, vocabulary, language, word analysis) and in math, and "Partial Mastery" in science and social studies.

Her grade reports vary in the school system. Sherokee's undated Student Information Profile in third grade reports a B in reading—at grade level. In math she earned a B, along with a note that problem-solving was a "weak skill." Her writing skill was average. The report shows Sherokee was not always a team player: "works well with others… needs improvement," the report reads. Yet on the Student's Scale Score Achievement Level, the Rutherford County School

District reveals her third-grade scores as "basic" in reading/language arts and science. Sherokee was "proficient" in math and "below proficient" in social studies.

So many different tests. Varying reports on all.

For her final report card, Sherokee made high B's and solid A's. The lowest grade is an 80. Her mom and Gran were so proud of her.

She was absent and late for class three times each, for a total of six attendance marks in third grade.

A problem arose that would now follow her every school year. In Sherokee's undated Student Information Profile under Behavior, the word "stealing" appears. Little things were still finding their way into her pockets: erasers, pencils, coins, hair ribbons, and other items that had little value. It was never the monetary value anyway. She just wanted pretty things, nice things, like everyone else seemed to have.

While her basic education skills were noted "at grade level," her people skills were sorely lacking. Yet another pattern had begun.

"I'm not going to school!" Sherokee raged. "I hate school! I hate it! I hate everybody!"

It was a familiar scene in the home. Rita was becoming weary of the battles. "Sherokee," Rita told her, "you have to go. You have to."

"If you make me go to school I'll kill myself!" she shrieked. "I will!"

Out of options, Rita says she made a telephone call. As Sherokee sat on the couch, fuming, a police officer knocked on the front door. Rita invited him in.

Sherokee's mouth fell open.

"What's going on here?" the cop asked.

"She's acting up again," Rita told the officer. "She says she'll kill herself if we make her go to school."

Sherokee's arms were crossed over her chest, her lower lip sticking out. "I will!" she told them. "If you keep making me go to school, I'll kill myself!"

Rita recalls the officer asking, "So, you really want to kill yourself?" The officer motioned for her to stand. "Stand up and turn around." The officer unsnapped a pair of handcuffs from his utility belt and told the little girl to place her hands behind her back. The handcuffs clicked around her wrists. She was then led away to sit in the back of a police car. With Rita following in her van, the cruiser drove off to TriStar StoneCrest Medical Center. Sherokee was taken to a room for suicidal patients.

"When she talked to the shrink, she told him she wasn't serious about it," Rita confides. "She just said it to get attention." Sherokee was released to Rita's care later that evening.

"She threatened suicide every time she didn't get her way, or she didn't want to do something," Rita says.

A Crisis Center was called several times in Sherokee's young life because she became a threat to herself. At one point the Center suggested Rita perform safety sweeps of the home and lock up all of the knives, scissors, and other sharp objects.

Sherokee had not yet passed the third grade.

CHAPTER 24

As they grew up, Sherokee and Shyloe grew close. They fought as sisters will, but even at such a young age, they stood up for one another as best they knew how. One of their favorite games was to pretend they were mermaids.

The little girls were splashing in the bathtub, and water was soaking the bathroom rug. It was bath time, and it was time to play mermaid. They pressed their feet together to pretend they had tails and splashed the bathwater at one another, giggling.

"I'm going to cast a mermaid spell!" Sherokee said ominously, holding up the soap and waving it as if it were a magic seashell. Her cotton-blonde hair was plastered to her head with soapy water.

"I'm going to cast a mermaid spell too, Sissy!" little Shyloe told her sister, splashing with her feet. "And then we will become ... mermaids!"

"Mermaids!" Sherokee declared, bringing the soap down with a splash. More water slopped over the edge of the tub.

"Mermaids!" Shyloe squealed.

Maybe it was one of their favorite games because Sherokee loved to swim, and Shyloe, although older, would follow Sherokee's lead. Maybe it was because mermaids have no problems; all they do is swim gracefully through the water, looking beautiful. Their world has no boundaries, for the ocean is big and there is always the shoreline for rest and more fun. Handsome, sweet men swoon over mermaids and write songs about their always elusive love. No one bothers these beautiful, intelligent creatures, no one disrespects them.

If danger appears, mermaids can just swim away to safety.

CHAPTER 25

On New Year's Eve 2010, Rita, Heather, Shyloe, and Sherokee arrived home to the house on Mitchell Avenue, still shaken up from a visit with Joe. Patriarch Joe had been admitted to Vanderbilt Hospital for numerous medical issues, including COPD and a weak heart.

As Sherokee opened the front door, Heather's dog scurried out of the house and pushed past her legs. The dog was followed by billowing smoke.

"Get away from the house!" Heather shouted at the girls. "Get away—don't go in!"

Sherokee grabbed Shy's hand and pulled her away, fearfully glancing back at the house as her mother and Gran went inside. Heart pounding, Sherokee watched the women enter the house, heard them shouting to one another.

As Rita opened the door to Shyloe's room, Heather did the first thing that came to mind: she turned the exhaust fan on. Both of them were forced out of the building. Coughing and fanning their faces, they joined the kids, who were already crying.

The fire was ruled an electrical fire caused by faulty wiring. It had started in the basement, moving on to Shyloe's room, then slowly travelled close to the dining area. It hit both Rita and Sherokee's rooms. Both of them lost a lot of things, including important mementoes.

Their landlord told them he was going to rebuild and renovate before he sold the property. The houses in the area had a value around $150,000. "You can't afford that," he told the Harrimans.

"He's right," Heather and Rita told one another. Now they would have to pack up what was left and find another place to rent. Salvaging what they could, the family gathered their belongings and left. The burned house would later be put on the market after complete renovations, selling for over $160,000.

Sherokee never healed completely. The fire had devastated her life: it took her things, uprooted her from her home, and made her feel scared and unsafe.

Long after the dark embers were cleaned away, long after the packing boxes were emptied, and the change of address cards were sent off, Sherokee still kept the tragedy close to her, tucked away in her head and heart. She had lost things that were dear to her. Fire had just bullied itself into her life and made her feel *so bad*.

CHAPTER 26

Sherokee was nine years old and entering fourth grade in August of 2010. This time, the little blonde girl would be sitting in a classroom at a different school. When the fire forced the family to move to another home, they also moved out of the Smyrna Elementary District. Now Sherokee and Rita were shopping for school supplies with a Stewartsboro Elementary School supply list in hand. She trailed behind Gran, who had to closely compare prices of pencils, paper, and folders to get the best bargains. Sherokee watched the other kids as their parents slung school supplies into their shopping carts with no apparent concern for price. Those kids wore new clothes and were excited and "helloing" other kids; their moms were stopping to chat with one another.

It was a big move, going to a new school. Sherokee saw it as only another chapter of her existence, a slave to the Board of Education's whims and demands. There would be more officials to judge her, tests to gauge her proficiency and intelligence, and more shuffling through the system that seemingly failed to understand or help her.

Teachers got mad because she was doing things she just could not stop, like losing interest in certain lesson plans, being short-tempered, and trying too hard to fit in with the "cool" kids. Principals and counselors just did not understand. Kids thought her strange. In her eyes, no one at school seemed too concerned over her happiness.

More bullying from fellow students.

More fights at home about her going to school.

As she thumbed through the folders featuring photographs of fuzzy kittens and puppies on the covers, she might of dared to hope this year would be better.

CHAPTER 27

Joseph Harriman's health steadily declined until he was bedridden and dependent on a colostomy bag and a trachea tube. His health record read like that of an old man who had lived life in anger and in poor health: he had been diagnosed with COPD, congestive heart failure, and diabetes. Now he lay in bed, wheezing noises escaping from his haggard face, his thin, silver hair mussed.

A photograph taken on Thanksgiving 2010 shows Joe looking worn and tired. Rita stares, unsmiling, into the camera. Sherokee's smile is one that has sadness behind it.

On December 4, Joe called Rita into the room. "Will you just sit a bit," he wheezed, "and just… just hold my hand?"

Rita had spent most of her time sitting by his bed when she was not cleaning his room, making him meals, or placing ice chips between his lips for hydration. She and Samantha changed and cleaned colostomy bags and handled his medical necessities. Now Rita sat next to Joe, holding his hand. She listened to his labored breathing, his heavy eyelids closed. "Dad," she finally whispered to him, "if you're holding on for me and the girls, we'll be okay." She squeezed his hand. "We'll be okay." She watched his face for any sign, then carefully set his hand down on the sheets and left the room.

It was young Sherokee who found him. "Gran," she reported to Rita, "Grandpa's cold and his air stopped." Her voice was trembling. "His lips are blue!"

Sherokee waited with her grandmother and an aunt for eight hours until the remains were taken away. Then Rita watched her husband of 42 years leave her forever. She could not cry, out of habit now. "It was hard on Sherokee," Rita remembers.

After her husband died, Rita "seemed to just shut down," recalls a family friend. "It was like she just folded." Rita refused to stay in the house where her husband died, so she moved to a little rental house in Smyrna. It was a three-bedroom, one-bath home with a large backyard. There was a park nearby called Mankin Park.

The little house was located on a busy, two-lane road. The houses along this road are small; the home owners and renters are not in the upper socioeconomic status of LaVergne. The inhabitants receive paychecks cut by fast-food franchises, factories, or government assistance agencies. Older manufactured homes dot the roadside. It is a mix of urban living and countryside, with a few cows and horses poking their heads over wire fences to watch the cars go by. The eclectic little neighborhood seems to be keeping new construction and the city's pace at bay.

They had had no money for a burial, so Rita had Joe's remains cremated. She plans to have the ashes placed at her feet when she is buried.

Joseph Harriman's ashes remain in a locked decorative box in the family room, still an overshadowing presence in the house.

CHAPTER 28

It seemed to Rita that Sherokee's behavior changed drastically after Joe's death. Where before her feelings and moods seemed to vacillate, now she could stay a terror. She had physically hurt cousins half her age, and she was striking out at Rita.

"Sherokee, I need you to clean your room," Rita would tell her.

"I'm not going to do it!"

"Clean your room!"

"No!"

Rita would find herself pushing Sherokee away from her, dodging the child's swinging fists. Sherokee's face would instantly redden, and her feet would deliver strong kicks at Rita.

"Sherokee, pick your stuff up off the living room floor."

"I'm not going to do it!"

If she was really angry, the threats of suicide would start.

"I'm going to kill myself!"

Then Rita would start in with a lecture on bad behavior, and her voice seemed to go round and round in Sherokee's mind; rather than sentences that made sense, Sherokee heard words and short phrases that fell on top of one another, scrambling around. She would later report to psychiatrists, "When people are talking, it gets jumbled in my head."

Shyloe's jabbering also grated on Sherokee's nerves. Shyloe had problems expressing herself still, and if asked a question she could go off on tangents before arriving at an answer. When this happened, Sherokee, pacing around the house, was clenching her teeth so hard her jaws ached.

The jaw-clenching was one of her "warning signs" that she was about to blow: sometimes she would pace. Sometimes she would sit and rock back and forth, her little hands curling into hard fists. Her face and throat burned crimson.

Trying to deep breathe never helped. "Time out" was useless.

Nothing could make Sherokee do something if she did not want to do it, no amount of arguing, pleading, or bribing. Threats never worked. "Sherokee, if you don't take a bath right now, you'll be grounded!"

She would only shrug, settling in with paper and crayons. "I don't care."

"Then you are grounded! No television, no—"

She would shrug, carefully selecting another crayon. "That's a joke," she replied smartly.

"You can't talk on the phone! You can't leave your room after you get home from school! No television for a week!"

Another shrug or short laugh. "I don't care."

Sometimes coloring helped calm her. Sometimes she would write, and listening to music seemed to sooth her.

Then there were serious outbursts, like when she would violently shove Shyloe into a wall or knock her down to the floor, just to make sure everyone saw who was in charge.

"Sherokee! Why did you hit your sister!"

"Shy's talking just gets on my nerves!" She would sit rocking, teeth grinding.

"Then leave the room! Go outside!" Now she was being told where to go! It was just crazy.

Deep inside, she knew she was never in control of anything. Not her feelings or her sadness, the mood swings, her household, the school system.

She certainly was not in control of her own body. Her stepfather had seen to that.

CHAPTER 29

After Joe died, Heather moved her things into her parent's home. "I know you don't want me here," she told Rita. Heather still could not get along with her mother. They circled one another warily, and soon the house was disrupted by their arguing. Unfortunately, neither adult had the skills to work through problems, whether past or present. They remained at opposite ends of the spectrum, and in that chasm, angry words and nasty accusations flew over and around the girls, who were caught in the middle.

When triggered, Sherokee would start her pacing the floor or just sit, rocking herself before she exploded. Sometimes she was able to escape into the world of drawing and coloring. Sometimes she escaped by staring at a television program, seemingly oblivious to the shouting and bickering.

"That's it!" an adult would rage at her. "Time out!"

"That's a joke."

It was maddening: nothing seemed to scare her into behaving. No one could make her do anything, and she was not above telling them so.

Rita, who was involved in church and took comfort in attending services, would take Sherokee to the Baptist church that she herself attended. Sherokee seemed to enjoy church. She loved to sing, so she participated in singing along with the congregation as they leafed through the hymn books. What she lacked in talent she made up for with enthusiasm. She was baptized in this church, and friends and fellow parishioners fussed over her, remarking what a pretty and sweet young lady she was.

But then she managed to steal money from the church missionary coffer. When she was confronted, Sherokee vehemently denied the theft, refusing to admit guilt even when the money was found in her pockets. Rita was mortified. This was far worse than when Sherokee was caught with stolen trinkets and candy at school, the origins of which could not be explained. Rita had no idea what to do about this: Sherokee stealing from the family and schoolmates was bad, but taking donations from the house of God was an abomination. To lie about it was added misery.

As she was lectured again for theft, Sherokee took the verbal blows as always: defiant, red-faced, seemingly bored with the whole mess.

The adults in her family believe that Sherokee did not understand why her grandfather had to leave her. She would remind them how she was feeling: everyone just bullied her and bossed her around. It wasn't fair he just left her here with this family. No one left in the house even cared about her.

It was clear that she missed him.

CHAPTER 30

With Sherokee, there was always so much going on. She wet the bed until she was 10 years old. It was embarrassing, to wet the bed like baby, to watch Gran having to strip the sheets and blankets for yet another wash. Finally a doctor prescribed Imipramine, an antidepressant also prescribed to treat bedwetting. Most times it helped.

She pretended as if she had a ton of friends: goofy, popular girls who loved to be around her. In reality, she had few. She unwittingly pushed people away when she manipulated them and threw tantrums.

But underneath the "bad kid" behavior was a soft-hearted, tender little girl who just wanted to be loved. She loved hugs and loved giving them, drawing hearts in pink crayon, her favorite color. She adored animals, particularly puppies. After she cooled down from a blow-up, she would always offer a sad and heartfelt apology. She said "I love you" quickly and easily, and meant it wholeheartedly.

"Sherokee wanted to be a good kid," says a family member who was well aware of the tantrums, the home security sweeps, and the battles between adults and child. "And she had to have a shell, to cover it all up."

And there was all that anger. It had to go somewhere.

She was caught setting a fire next to the family car, setting a lighted match to a piece of paper and watching the burning paper fall to the ground, curling under that elusive yellow flame. Another time she was caught lighting the living room curtains, trying to set them ablaze.

Sometime later, Sherokee would admit some of the fires were set with the intention to burn the house down with all occupants inside. When asked why, Sherokee explained, "I want to kill Gran. I want to kill Mom. I want to kill Shy. I want everyone dead."

"I don't think she had anyone she could talk to," confides a family member.

"She never said why [she set fires]," Shyloe adds. "She just did it."

Sherokee's grades had wavered across the board as she made her way to the fourth grade. As she completed this year, Sherokee left a telling school record. She had missed four days of school and was tardy on eight separate days. Her "outstanding" grades had dropped to "satisfactory." Her grades in reading, social studies, and science fell between C's and D's. She did better in math and language, but now spelling remained the sole A grade.

Her Student's Scale Score Achievement Level in the Rutherford County School District mirrors the letter grades: she had "below basic" achievement levels in reading/ language arts, science, and social studies. Sherokee was graded "basic" in math.

There are no written detailed records of parental conferences in her fourth-grade school file, only a "yes" indicating a conference on the Rutherford County School District log.

Despite her grades, the school system passed her into fifth grade. She was just one of the 16.1 million elementary school students[9] shuffled through a system that was under-funded, over-budgeted, and doing the best it could with little resources.

Her fifth-grade year started in August of 2010. A prevocational skills checklist completed on September 6,

---

9. U.S. Census Bureau, March 2001 report, *School Enrollment in the U.S.*

2010, revealed that Sherokee could perform basic tasks, but she was slow-moving when it came to preparing and continuing her work. She did not respect other people's property rights nor did she behave appropriately: she became angered when disappointed and felt blameless for her actions.

Despite her problems in academia, Sherokee loved being with friends at school. She giggled and gossiped with friends, helloing people in the halls. Her few buddies knew her as a sweet little girl who loved drawing. While her moods seemed to shift often, she was still a good friend to talk to; she kept secrets and was always there to listen.

She said goodbye to fifth grade in 2011. She would still be attending class at Rock Springs Middle School that fall. Still, it was summertime, her favorite season, which meant no school and no bullies. Sherokee wrote of the season:

Summer you are an awesome season
You look like sun, sand, and swimming pools
You sound like waves, children playing, and teens talking
You are like a dream to me
I can swim and play outside

But all was not idyllic. At first Rita believed it was a case of absent-mindedness. She thought she had put the few dollars in her purse, but then there was that $5 bill and some change she had left on her dresser. Now it had disappeared. Money was so tight in the household, and every dollar counted. It was strange the money she was so careful to save just went missing from her purse and her room so easily.

At the same time, Sherokee came home from the store with little trinkets and things she thought were pretty. Nail polish. Hair clips. Cheap little bracelets. Once she was able to buy herself some ice cream. It did not take long to learn Sherokee was nicking money from her Gran. Some coins, a dollar, maybe more if it was available and she had a moment alone in the room.

Punishment did not stop it. Sherokee so wanted those pretty things. She wanted trivial things the family could not afford, and she was going to get them any way she could.

CHAPTER 31

In late October 2011, Michael "Mike" Edwards (no relation to Mack) was seeking someone special, someone to share his life with, and he did what so many people do to find companionship: he tried an online dating site. That was when he found a woman named Heather Harriman.

They talked online for some time. Heather found someone who could make her laugh; she sometimes practically fell out of her chair at his witticisms. Mike liked talking to her: she was interesting, and they had long online conversations. She was forthright and honest. He gave her his phone number. "If you decide you don't want to talk to me anymore, I understand and you can go on," he told her. She appreciated a man who respected her feelings, who understood she was afraid of being hurt. She could talk about her daughters, and he was interested in a safe way. Mike, an Oklahoma native, loved her Southern accent.

After many conversations online and on the phone, they decided it was time to meet in person. Their first date was on New Year's Eve, the last night of 2011. Heather introduced him to her kids when he came over. Sherokee was skittish and untrusting. Mike understood and kept his distance.

They count January 16, 2012, as the official day they began dating seriously.

At last Heather found someone who loved her unconditionally, someone who would stick around when times were tough, a hard worker with a wonderful sense of humor and a big heart. Mike was sensitive and strong. Like her, he loved animals. He was a Star Wars fan and dreamed of driving a Lamborghini car some day. He truly doted on Heather. He understood her, never judging her. Everyone makes big mistakes, he told her: it's what you do with it that really counts.

Mike moved into the home with Heather, Rita, and the girls in September 2012. Shyloe and Sherokee shared a small bedroom. Heather and Mike's room as well as Rita's bedroom were on the opposite end of the short hallway. It was a home that was more cozy than cramped, with a living room, a kitchen, and a nice-sized yard in back. In the evenings, they would sit on the front stone steps and watch the traffic whiz past.

Mike brought a sparkle that had always been absent in Heather's eyes, that light that had been hidden by sadness and hurt. She would laugh at his one-liners so hard she had to wipe tears from her eyes, but they were happy tears this time.

Mike was working a blue-collar job not too far from where they lived, putting in many hours on shift work. He pitched in to help with bills and taking care of the house. And he worked with the girls to let them know he loved them.

The latter was so important to Sherokee.

Mike remembers one day when he was with the girls in his car. Sherokee and Shyloe were so impressed with the car's sunroof. They smiled and giggled, stretching their hands upward to catch the wind, dipping their fingers to move with the breeze. Sherokee rode along in the front seat, the breeze lifting the edges of her long blonde hair. She quietly watched everything go past, deep in thought.

Mike recalls what she said. "Then she turned to look at me and asked, 'Are you the kind of man that would touch a child?'"

Mike was taken back, but he was honest. "No," he assured her.

She thought about it, turning to gaze again out of the car window. "Good."

And he recalls how, around six months into his relationship with Heather, Sherokee shyly approached him. "Can I call you 'Daddy?'"

Mike's heart overflowed as he told her easily, "If that's what you want to, then it's okay."

Mike, with his quick wit and easy smile, became "Daddy" to both girls. To this day, he refuses to be called a stepfather. He playfully began calling Sherokee "Chickie," a play on her existing nickname, Chik.

When the church had a father-daughter banquet, Mike proudly dressed up to escort the girls. When Shyloe went to a prom designed for the special education students, Mike drove her to school to get ready. Shy had her makeup done by a group of volunteers from the cosmetology classes, and she wore a pretty dress. Mike waited patiently outside in the car for her, posting on Facebook about how happy he was and how proud he was of Shyloe. He believed in the girls, and he believed in Heather.

With Mike's encouragement, Heather started her own business, a cleaning company. She had finally found someone who respected her, truly loved her, and was a good provider. He assisted with the cleaning company until he obtained work at a local manufacturing company. Mike worked hard on the swing shift, helping around the house, spending time with his family, and catching sleep when he could. A loving daddy, he could also be a disciplinarian when needed.

"He is a hard worker," observes a family member. "He is patient and does a lot of the housework."

But some things had not changed for Heather. "[She] is still angry at the world," confides a good friend. "Or maybe she's angry at herself."

Maybe Heather continued to beat herself up over the way she had treated her daughters. Maybe the anger could stem from the fact that Shyloe and Sherokee were still being raised in the very household that Heather had run away from and still could not seem to escape.

Sherokee loved having Mike in her life, but she was still having problems in school. She continued attending Rock Springs Middle School. Medical records show she was seen twice in the nurse's office, November 3 and 4, 2012, for head lice. She was in fifth grade.

The taunts by her peers started in class and in the halls.

"Eew, you stink!"

"Watch out—she's dirty!"

She still hated school and hated being called names and made fun of by the other kids. She tried her best to get out of going, but feigning illnesses and ambiguous complaints only worked for so long. She missed nine days in the second quarter, eight days in the third, and two days in the last quarter of the school year.

Her grades for the school year 2011–2012 showed mostly B's.

Again, she took the TCAP tests at the end of the school year. Sherokee did well in her best subject, math. Her reading/language arts scores ranged from "below basic" to "basic." Her social studies scores were "below proficient." And in science her grades were poor across the board: "below basic."

Still, she was passed on to the next grade.

"It's that 'no child left behind' [system]," Rita Harriman would explain later, "and it's crap."

CHAPTER 32

Rita and Heather admit they continued to fight, and in such a small house everyone was privy to what was said. Many of their arguments centered around Sherokee's hygiene.

Rita recalled what happened when she asked Heather to make Cherokee bathe following a medical exam during which Rita was mortified to learn that her granddaughter was not cleaning herself properly. Heather did not respond well.

"You just want their fuckin' money!" she shouted. When her mother told her to watch her language, Heather responded with more heat. "It's my life! I'm an adult!"

Heather says she told her mother exactly what she had told Joe about the words she chose to use. "I'm a grown woman! I'll fucking talk the way I want to fucking talk!"

Rita pointed at Sherokee. "She has to stop hitting and kicking!"

And now Heather's voice could be heard outside the house with one of her usual accusations about why Rita did not like Sherokee. "She! Is! Just! Like! Me!"

The argument would end with Rita closing herself off in her room, and Heather lighting another cigarette, both women secretly fighting tears of frustration. The adults were not the only frustrated occupants in the little house.

Sherokee seemed to soak up the anger, plus she had her own demons festering. Why was Gran in charge? Why were they always yelling and fighting? She was sick and tired of being caught in the middle. Mama blamed Gran for

Sherokee's bad behavior. Gran said it was her mother's fault. And in between, it seemed to her that Shyloe was always shoving Sherokee out of the way, getting so much attention.

As they grew, Shyloe still had the better part of her grandmother's attention because of the girl's learning disability. It took a lot of patience and time to work with Shyloe. If they wanted her to pay attention, they had to hold her face, force her to look into their eyes, and give instructions slowly and carefully. Shyloe had to be told how to do so many things, such as to refrain from chugging down a soda or answering a question by yammering about unrelated subjects. Her thoughts flew around her like birds, sailing this direction and that or straight up in the air. Shyloe would hit herself in frustration or bang her head into the walls. Sometimes she would bite into her own arm, hard enough to leave a bruise. It was so difficult for her to express her feelings. She could talk nonstop, acting much younger than her age, though she also could be quite introspective. Her memory was unshakable. She would give quick hugs, and she could be so polite. She could read all day but had no comprehension of what the words meant, but she could watch a television program and repeat every detail. It took a lot of energy and patience to work with Shyloe, which meant a lot of time. Sherokee resented this: in her eyes, Shy got *all* the attention.

Between having to care for her ailing husband before his death and her needy grandchildren, all while trying to raise the kids on their meager salary, Gran Rita had had little time to play and less attention to spend on Sherokee. Then, once widowed, she lacked the heart for so many things, emotionally destitute at Joseph's death.

One of their biggest ongoing arguments was about Sherokee's school attendance. She continued to fight most mornings about going to school. Still fuming, she would get on the school bus. Only a few hours later, Rita would receive a telephone call that Sherokee was in the nurse's office, claiming that she did not feel good.

She was spiraling again, lashing out one moment, being sweet and loving the next. "I know my mom doesn't love me," a family member recalls Sherokee saying. "I know Gran doesn't like me." Perhaps she felt it was true, or perhaps it was an act to gain sympathy. Sometimes it was hard to tell.

Her best friend Katie understood that Sherokee felt trapped. Sherokee saw the school system as one big bully, where she had a hard time relating to students, schoolwork, and the administration. She found no solace at home. Her bedroom seemed like "Shy's room." Gran spent a lot of time in her own room, and Mama and Daddy's room was their own. There was just nowhere to go, nowhere to just be alone to sort things out or try to control the thoughts and emotions. She kept everything so pent up that when she did show how she felt, she exploded.

Katie recalls one time when she and Sherokee were on the computer and Sherokee happened to look out the window. A stray dog was stepping of the curb just as a car came speeding up on the busy, two-lane road. The dog dodged just in time. "Oh my GOD!" Sherokee let out a scream and ran outside, Katie behind her.

The dog had escaped, but Sherokee was devastated. She began to sob uncontrollably, choking back sobs. "He– he–" And then she could not catch her breath. Her tear-stained face reddened, her breath became a wheeze, and she slumped to the ground, the front of her shirt soaked with tears.

Katie tried to get her to calm down. "Sherokee, it's okay! See! He didn't get hit! He didn't get hit!"

Sherokee was so upset a neighbor came out of an adjoining house. "Is she okay?" the woman asked.

Katie assured the neighbor that her friend was fine, just terribly upset. She sat with Sherokee until her best friend felt better. Katie shook her head. Sherokee just could not stand the thought of animals hurting, particularly dogs, despite the fact that she had fatally injured her own family pet.

Tears and anger were always right under the surface. When things were not going as she wanted, Sherokee made sure everyone knew how miserable she was. "I hate you! I hate my life!" she would shriek when she was not allowed to do something she wanted to do. "Why does everyone hate me! It's not fair!"

Not long afterward, though, there would be sincere apologies and, "I love you," all around. She did love her family, and they all knew it. But why she would shout about how much she hated everyone, no one was really sure. How could such a sweet girl turn into an angry terror so easily?

Despite Sherokee's perception that life, in general, was just never fair, there were many good times. A family friend repaired and refurbished two bicycles, and Sherokee and Shyloe would ride them through the yard, giggling and calling out to one another. Their mother took them to the park to run and play on the swing sets. The girls spent time with relatives, playing with their cousins and having sleepovers. Katie was a staple in Sherokee's life, and Shyloe loved Katie, too.

Sherokee had a few good friends, and they always had fun. There was music and dancing, mooning over television and movie stars, cute boy bands, and singers. Giggling over nothing and everything. It was great fun to sing along with music. Her uncle had a karaoke and DJ business, and Sherokee was not shy about performing, holding the microphone while looking at the song's words on the monitor. Everyone always clapped for her afterward, and she would shyly grin, revealing how much she loved the validation.

Heather always made sure to give hugs and tell the kids she loved them every chance she could, and the girls responded in kind. She recalls how Sherokee shared many secrets, because Sherokee knew Heather would not be judgmental. Heather was trying hard to be the mom she wanted to be and had always wanted, although she did slip sometimes, particularly when the girls tried her patience. Mike was also quick to return hugs and an "I love you!" He made the girls giggle by being silly and fun.

They grew up playing the quintessential children's board games Candyland and Chutes and Ladders. Sherokee loved to play Yahtzee, a dice game that relies on numbers and critical thinking, which her grandfather taught her to play when she was seven years old. She was so good at the game, it was difficult to get anyone to play because she always won. A difficult game where she excelled! Sherokee loved Yahtzee.

CHAPTER 33

"I'll drink that beer if you give me a fucking cigarette."

The cell-phone video was clear, albeit shaky. Sherokee grins and looks mischievously at her friend, who is holding the phone. She did not realize her friend was actually recording her. Worried for Sherokee, the friend eventually shared the video with school officials, who contacted Rita and Heather.

Her family was already aware that Sherokee would sneak cigarettes. At one point she stole a pack of Heather's cigarettes just to crunch the pack in her hands until tobacco flakes poured out. Heather wondered if it was a ploy to try to keep her from smoking or just plain acting out.

Desperate for attention and craving unconditional love, Sherokee's acting out did not always receive attention, so she had resorted to cursing. Any attention would do, and spewing curse words became the norm. That it angered Gran made it all the more better. Some attention was better than none at all. At least she was being noticed.

After a while, even cursing was not doing the trick.

She was in fifth or sixth grade when something much worse happened, Rita confides. Despite her problems with learning, Shyloe has excellent recall, and she shared the details of a scary incident.

Sherokee and two of her younger cousins were in the garage, and the little ones watched her as she carefully walked around the riding lawn mower, sizing it up. The little kids stared at the bigger girl, partially in fascination and curiosity, partially in fear.

Sherokee knelt down and the blade to the pocketknife snapped open.

"Where did you get that!" one of the little cousins asked, horrified.

"It's Grandpa's," Sherokee told her casually. "I took it from his room." There was a SNAP, and gas began flooding over the garage floor. The smaller girls stepped back, noses wrinkling as the smell permeated the small garage.

Sherokee cut her eyes at the girls, glaring at each of them. "If you tell anyone," she warned, "I'll kill you."

The youngsters knew she meant it. Sherokee had hit them in the past, had shoved them and knocked them down on purpose. When she was mad, it was best to clear the room. They kept the secret as long as they dared.

"Who cut the gas line!" Mike's voice could be heard throughout the house as he barged into the room. "Who did it!"

Shyloe's big, blue eyes widened at this news. "It wasn't me," she told him.

"Sherokee!" Mike's face was red. He was furious. "Did you do it!"

"No!" she shouted back.

"Did you cut the gas line on Grandpa's mower?"

She glared at him and insisted coolly, "No. I didn't."

Shyloe remembers, "She wouldn't admit it. But we all knew it was her."

Another time Shyloe watched silently as Sherokee unlocked the pocket knife's blade. *Click.*

Sherokee begin to run deliberate, jagged cuts down the length of the mattress on her bed. Then Sherokee looked over at her sister.

"Sissy, if you tell mama," Sherokee promised, "I'll *hurt* you."

"I believed her," Shyloe says now. They were already physically fighting, with slaps, kicks, and shoves. They had hurt one another more than a few times in fist fights. Heather resorted to keeping them physically apart in the house.

Some fights continued to turn physical between Sherokee and Rita. Sherokee would shove, punch, and kick Rita when they argued, just as she shoved and slapped her sister, and their arguments turning into brawls, with bodies slamming against the walls of the little house.

"One time I hit her in the face," Shyloe explains casually, "really good."

In between, Sherokee raged at herself. "I hate myself!"

"I'm just going to kill myself!"

"Nobody loves me!"

Sometimes she just said it, hoping to turn the tide in her favor, to get what she wanted, like a cell phone. All the kids around Sherokee had cell phones, and they could text and Tweet and listen to music. They could check their Facebook. A kid without a cell phone just was not part of the "normal" crowd, much less the popular bunch.

It became a young person's status symbol: the better your phone, the better you were.

Heather's heart ached for her daughter. She knew how badly Sherokee wanted to fit in, but she also knew that finances were stretched, and the bare necessities were more important than being able to text people and play games. Because the contract plans were so expensive, the family purchased prepaid wireless service.

Wanting desperately to have her own cell phone, and wanting to fit in so badly, Sherokee resorted to what she always did when she wanted nice things. She stole a one, and of course, was caught and had to give it back to the owner. And of course, her peers did not consider her "cool" at all: they now saw her as a thief and a liar. The shame and frustration fueled her pain, which turned into even more anger.

CHAPTER 34

The sounds and shapes came at night, and when she heard or saw them, she would yank the covers up over her head, quaking in her bed. There was someone outside, rustling around. Sherokee could hear them; along with the pounding of her heart in her ears, she could hear them through the window.

Sometimes she could see them. A slight, quick shadow across the room. She would squeeze her eyes closed so tight the muscles around her eyeballs would sting. Then she would slowly open them, the room a bit more dusky from the self-imposed blackness. Maybe they would be there. Maybe they would be gone. She had to chance a peek...

Nothing there. Just the walls of her bedroom, the sounds of—

What was that!

Sherokee Harriman had a difficult time sleeping every night. Even on the good days, it was hard to settle off to a comfortable slumber. Finally, exhaustion would take over, and she would toss in a fitful attempt at rest. Just like so many other victims of abuse and PTSD, Sherokee Harriman was plagued by nightmares. They would follow her throughout her short life.

It was impossible to know what they wanted or what they were doing, but the nightmares were there. Always in the shadows, they gave themselves away with the slightest sound and movement.

Always at night.

They were just waiting there for her.

She would have to stay vigilant until her eyes burned with sleep. Then sleep came, but with more disturbing images.

CHAPTER 35

Sherokee was seeing a counselor named Joycie, a professional who came to the home to talk with her and her sister. It was obviously not changing Sherokee's behaviors, and Joycie sat down with Rita to suggest that treatment go a step further.

Sherokee's fascination setting fires was out of control. She was physically and verbally abusive. She acted like the whole therapy thing was one big pain in the ass, which Joycie saw as avoidance. Sherokee could talk for hours about hair, makeup, and music, but she shut down when exploring her own feelings.

She wanted to fit in so desperately that she was stealing things that she thought would make her pretty or popular. Other kids and adults did not seem to understand why she was stealing; they just knew her as a thief.

Her violence had gotten so out of hand that legal authorities had become involved: Sherokee was now on probation because she had hit Rita.

Sherokee had such a loving nature, but the negative behavior now far outweighed the good. She had a sweet smile and was blossoming into a pretty girl. Sherokee loved giggling and playing, wanted boys to notice her, and lent an ear to whoever needed to talk. But having fun could be so difficult: she was having such a struggle to keep the anger tamped down that, once it exploded, it was like a geyser.

Something had to be done. Home visits with Joycie were not helping the pretty girl with the beautiful smile. So the counselor suggested something more drastic.

Oak Plains is a 20-acre facility located between Clarksville and Ashland City, Tennessee. It specializes in psychiatric residential treatment for children ages 5 to 17, Joycie explained to Rita. "They have a school, therapy groups, counseling, and would prescribe and regulate her medication." Joycie answered Rita's questions about the cost and the insurance that would cover it. In a desperate act of not knowing what to do and being unable to help this child, her grandmother placed ten-year-old Sherokee in Oak Plains.

Sherokee walked through the front door of the one-story, light yellow stucco building called Oak Plains Academy. She was only about a 90-minute drive from LaVergne, but it felt like being on another planet. The calendar read August 27, 2012.

Rita Harriman signed her in and completed a stack of paperwork. She looked over at Sherokee, her mouth set in a thin line. The little girl's eyes were bloodshot, and her face was chapped from all the crying she had done from the minute they had gotten into the van and left home.

"You hate me! This is why you're doing this!" Sherokee had howled in between the floods of tears. "If you loved me you wouldn't make me go there!" Then she would change, becoming contrite. "Please don't make me go! I promise if you don't make me go, I won't start any more fires… I won't smoke… I won't drink— I'll… I'll go to school!" She choked on her sobs, then her red-rimmed eyes narrowed. She punched the van console. "Why do you all hate me! I know mom and dad hate me! Why are you sending me here! I hate everybody!"

Now Rita was seated in the quiet office, speaking with an admissions specialist, answering questions and signing documents. Sherokee was also answering questions. She admitted she was at Oak Plains because of her pyromania, the stealing and lying, and refusing to do chores. Explaining why she acted so bad, she told the woman in the admitting office, "My sister's dad abused us."

Rita gave them a history of Sherokee's young life, including how she was a happy little girl initially, then her behaviors changed. She wondered if it was because of Joe's death. "She doesn't have friends," Rita explained flatly.

Sherokee admitted to having her first cigarette at age ten, swiped from the pack of one of Heather's friends. It was the sole time she had smoked, she told them. She was not using or experimenting with drugs.

The specialist would note that Heather moved in with Rita after Joe's death, and that Rita felt Heather was spending too much time with her boyfriend.

"What do you believe Sherokee's treatment goal should be?" the specialist asked.

Rita explained, "We want Sherokee to deal with her anger and stop stealing. She needs to stop setting fires and stop hurting people."

When Sherokee was asked the same question, she was truthful. "Stop stealing, setting fires, and lying." Sherokee told them she liked swimming and volleyball. She loved to sing and do artwork, and she liked board games. She still excelled at Yahtzee. She was friendly and sat quietly. Her clothes and skin were clean, but closer inspection would reveal the head lice that made her scalp itch.

"What do you want to be when you grow up, Sherokee?" the specialist asked.

"I think I would like to be a police officer," was her answer.

Finally, it was time to say goodbye. Sherokee headed into the halls of Oak Plains, and Rita walked stiffly through the parking lot in the opposite direction. Part of her soul felt saddened that it came to this. The other part of her felt relief because now Sherokee could get help.

Rita refused to allow herself to cry.

Diagnosis (Acute symptoms): Post Traumatic Stress Disorder (PTSD), (Oppositional Defiant Disorder (ODD)

Per the Tennessee Department of Education guidelines, this young lady would meet certifying standards … to be labeled ED (Emotionally Disturbed).
—Oak Plains Academy Psychological Evaluation of Sherokee Rose

Harriman, 9/1/12

CHAPTER 36

Sherokee was shown the patient rooms, each with cinderblock walls painted in relaxing colors, and each with a bunk bed and a desk on either side. A rectangular window, level with the top bunk, allowed the shifting Tennessee weather to peep in between the beds.

Patients were placed on a "level" system, she was told, where good behavior moved children up to levels that offered privileges, and bad behavior meant losing a level and a privilege. The first was "Coyote Level;" "Lion Level" was the highest level she could reach. Sherokee agreed that reaching "Lion" should be her goal.

On August 30, a clinical therapist completed a preliminary treatment plan for Sherokee. Sherokee told her that she had problems with her anger, lying, stealing, and starting fires. She told the therapist she was smart. "I'm good at art," she smiled shyly. The therapist noted both individual and group therapy would begin immediately, and family therapy should be arranged.

Sherokee explained how, when people started talking to her, their words "are all jumbled in my head." She paid attention to the questions and smiled, and the therapist noted she was a pretty little girl. "I've seen things and heard things," Sherokee admitted somberly, telling about the nightmares and the hallucinations experienced at night.

Her traumas were listed, including the sexual abuse, her mother's neglect, the house fire, and the death of her grandfather, according to the Oak Plains assessments. There was also the possibility of "sexually inappropriate behavior."

Sherokee was also given five 20-item questionnaires to assess anxiety, depression, anger, self-concept, and disruptive behavior. They were collectively called the *Beck Youth Inventories for Children and Adolescents.* She was also given other tests, to include the *Kaufman Brief Intelligence Test.* During this process, Sherokee was lackadaisical about taking what she perceived as just more stupid tests, just like in regular school. "My eyes hurt," she complained. "I can't see anything 'cause everything's blurry." She covered one eye with her hand. "I see better like this, though," although her vision test revealed she had 20/24 vision.

Her test answers indicated she was not trying, nor was she making an effort to think anything through. It was decided to perform another variety of tests after her medication was stabilized.

Test results revealed symptoms typical of a child who had experienced sexual abuse: PTSD, anger, distrust, and suspiciousness. She was clinically depressed and had symptoms indicative of such: poor relationship skills, chronic distress, lack of self esteem, and emotional and functional problems. Sherokee was a child coping with problems most adults would find overwhelming.

"She had a horrible, short life," a family member would say later.

Despite the diagnosis, Sherokee saw herself as an outgoing, friendly girl who was a follower rather than a leader, a kid who longed for relationships but because of her problems and behaviors, she was just unable to maintain them. She wanted friendships and boyfriends, but her emotional disruptions made it all impossible. She knew she had problems, she told the doctors, but she could not control them.

Sherokee was a sad, mixed-up little girl.

The professionals used the American Psychiatric Association's Diagnostic and Statistical Manual of Mental Disorders (DSM) to report Sherokee's Diagnostic Impression. The DSM-IV organized each psychiatric diagnosis into five dimensions (axes) relating to different aspects of disorder or disability. Sherokee's record in September 2012 read in part:

Axis I (used for psychological diagnostic categories except mental retardation and personality disorder):
Post Traumatic Stress Disorder secondary to early sexual trauma (PTSD)
Oppositional Defiant Disorder (ODD)
Mood Disorder
Psychotic Disorder
ADHD traits-?
Axis II:
Borderline intellectual functioning

The Diagnostic Impression also read:

Ongoing chronic conflict within the home and school some of this being internal possibly historically evident and indicative of a very disturbed young lady at the present time.

Sherokee's psychological problems were the reason she was not doing well in school; they were also harming her emotional growth. The child psychologist recommended ongoing therapy, including a sexual abuse survivor's group and family therapy.

The facility's doctors placed Sherokee on medication and regulated activities designed to help her cope with her psychological and emotional problems. When she came to Oak Plains, 50 mg of Seroquel XR and 50 mg of Zoloft flowed through her system in an effort to stabilize her moods. In September, she was placed on multivitamins and on 5 mg of Abilify (Aripiprazole), an anti-psychotic medication which changes the actions of the brain's chemicals. Abilify is used to treat depression and mood disorders in children (including aggression, tantrums, and mood swings). She was also prescribed 50 mg of the anticonvulsant Trazodone (Trimethadione). Sherokee was treated for lice, and she saw a dentist for teeth cleaning.

Sherokee received her "Coyote Level 2" in early September.

Soon the Zoloft was decreased and the Seroquel stopped. Sherokee stayed on the Abilify and Trazodone.

Sherokee was not under- or overweight for her age, but she was growing up on a diet common to families in the lower socioeconomic ranks, one that was full of starches, fats, and chemicals. The Oak Plains team, in an attempt to get her physically well, had a multi-disciplinary approach that included diet. She was given double portions of food together with nutritional supplement drinks full of proteins to get her body back to health. But she began refusing the supplement drinks. "That makes me throw up," she told staff. "I'm not taking it anymore."

Students received awards, a single sheet of paper with a stock photo taken from a website. She received several "Best-Safe Award" sheets. She received a "Team Player Award" from one of her teachers. For the first weeks in December, she was "Student of the Week." And she received an award for "Leadership" three times.

A teacher checklist shows Sherokee as being cooperative, enjoying and taking part in class, and doing well working independently and in a group. Her communication appears to have improved within class and socially. She was not a leader, but she was a solid part of a team. The only negative note that accompanied this report was "speaks softly."

The Oak Plains Academy school features small classrooms where one-on-one instruction is available. Students receive personable attention needed to complete schoolwork. Her grades reflected the extra attention. Initially, her grades were between D's and B's. After some time, her report card showed all B's with the exception of physical education, reading, and spelling where she made A's. Even in her worst subject, social studies, a proud Sherokee showed off a B grade. But sometimes she would become frustrated with herself and just stop trying. Shutting down remained one of her coping skills.

Sherokee also took a Forced Choice Reinforcement Test; its purpose was to reveal "individual reinforcement preferences." Her scores revealed that Sherokee sought adult and peer approval and "consumable rewards" on a high level, but her highest score was for "independent rewards," meaning she felt best about schoolwork when she felt good about herself.

Sherokee attended therapy groups and individual therapy sessions. She struggled to understand her triggers, her feelings, and understanding why she was acting out. It was so difficult to get her to open up. She did not understand that a correction for behavior was not a comment on her personally; adults could tell her "no," but it did not mean she was disliked. By October, she was gaining some insight into why she was so angry and upset.

"My mom and Gran put me in the middle," she told the therapist. "I don't like it: why is Gran in charge? Why does she have to be the boss of me?" She had once thought about moving away from Gran and living with Heather and her boyfriend. Then she would decide it was best to be with Gran. "Why can't my mom can't always be with me?"

"Does she work?"

"Yes! But I want her to be with me!"

"But Sherokee, doesn't she have to work so she can buy food, and clothes, and pay her bills?"

Still Sherokee insisted. "But I want her to be with me!"

At Oak Plains, she did get to visit with her mom, Gran, and even Mike. Visitation was allowed only on weekends for just two hours. Her family made the drive to see her; they played board games with her and just talked.

She seemed to be progressing, but in early October she was disciplined for acting out. On October 15, she was carefully monitored because she had threatened to harm herself; monitoring lasted for two days until she was determined safe.

"I am so proud of you, Sherokee! You are doing so well!" a staff member told her in November; indeed, she was also proud of herself. She had stopped stealing and was able to control herself. She was continually learning coping skills, but at this point seemed to be interested in modifying her behavior and was striving to make changes. Her level moved up to "Cougar 2" in early November. Records show she was at "Eagle 1" just 15 days later. In just a few days, she made "Eagle 2."

It seemed her family was working on getting better. Rita and Heather agreed the shouting had to stop and that placing Sherokee in the middle was doing everyone harm. They were going to work on this problem together and individually.

Still, it was so hard to not shout, because sometimes this felt like the only way to be heard. Lifestyle changes were so hard to break. Old anger was so difficult to just let go. There was so much left unspoken, so many skeletons scratching at closet doors.

CHAPTER 37

It seemed to Sherokee that the doctors and the psychiatrists and everyone in between wanted her to talk about what Shyloe's father did to her. They just kept wanting her to talk: talk about how she felt, what scared her, why she was so angry. She simply was not interested in sharing.

Her counselors had her playing therapeutic games to help her transition into a safe environment where it was okay to talk about the really bad things. Sherokee liked the games until they took a turn where she had to open up or she knew where input was expected. *Nope, not today*. More fun to just play the game and not think about bad things.

Sherokee felt like she was doing well with the other kids, and she liked the school at Oak Plains. But it was so hard when the class was supposed to be doing work that required imagination and discipline. Math and science came easy. The rules were set in those concrete subjects.

One thing she did keep repeating was that she loved her family. Despite the fighting and arguing, she loved them all deeply. No one doubted that. She did not mind talking about how much she missed her grandfather, or about how the house fire took her things and made life seem so unsafe.

But she did *not* want to answer any questions nor discuss what happened to her when she was three. Sherokee did not want to discuss why she set fires or stole things. Sometimes she would just change the subject. Other times, she clammed up, her hands together in her lap, eyes focused on the floor.

The bad things still haunted her at night. People were outside of her bedroom, she was convinced, milling around, just waiting to get to her. There were the sounds and the shadows. And then...

What was that!

Her vision would blur from staring so hard at windows and doors. She kept the covers pulled to her chin, eyes darting from the walls to the corners. Breathing was difficult; it came in short, raspy puffs.

Nighttime was so dark. Anyone could slip into her room, and it would be hard to catch them. Best to keep vigilant.

CHAPTER 38

She was still adamant about not discussing the details of certain traumas in her life. Sometimes she would sit, rocking in place. Try as they might, therapists just could not get her to open up when she was like this.

Sometimes, Sherokee would tell staff that she thought this Oak Plains business was just a bully, making her do things she did not want to do and talk about things that she did not want to talk about. And if she didn't play by the rules, they were just so mean to her. Talk to me about this, they would say, tell us about that. You can't do this, stop doing that. On and on. So many demands.

So, despite her successes at the school, she decided to escape. In early December, Sherokee was caught trying to run away. After her return to the facility, she was carefully observed and monitored for four days until she was declared safe.

By mid-December, she was at "Eagle 3." Then in early February of 2013, a strange dynamic took shape. At that time, Sherokee was allowed to go home twice on passes. The passes allowed her to practice the skills she learned in the Oak Plains. It seemed she was truly working on her behaviors, although healing progress was slow in some areas.

While at home on passes, Sherokee was polite and did well with anger management. But once back behind the doors of Oak Plains, she was once again volatile, refusing to obey rules and requests. "Fuck you, you stupid bitch!" she would snap at nurses. "You asshole! You bitch!" She swore at other students in class and in the hallways. If there was any comeback, they would be at it, Sherokee hurling expletives at whoever got in her way. One staff member was physically hit; Sherokee attacked a fellow patient, grabbing the person by the neck and squeezing. Sherokee blamed everyone but herself for the bad behavior.

"Well, they should've stayed out of my way," she insisted. "She pushed my buttons."

"So it isn't your fault? Was it a good idea to hurt someone?"

No answer. Silence.

At home, while she made visits, her mother and grandmother had continued to argue, and no real rules were set for her. At Oak Plains, she had stability and guidance. At home, nothing had changed.

Sherokee admitted to hitting her sister during a fight at home during a pass, and yes, she was bullying the kids into fighting on the unit where she was staying at Oak Plains.

"Your discharge date has been extended twice, making your stay here longer," she was told. "Don't you think your behavior has caused this?"

Not her fault. Someone else made her. Everyone hates her. She always had the same excuses for her bad behavior, or else she would just stop talking and stare at the floor. And the insomnia and the nightmares were still there, causing her to toss and turn with worry and fear. The doctors prescribed 9 mg of melatonin to help her sleep.

There was one night when Sherokee was caught staying up past bedtime. The security officer was making rounds in the halls of Oak Plains when the guard heard noises. An investigation found a naked Sherokee under a blanket with another female patient. Later, Sherokee would confide the details to Heather, and Heather has kept that private.

Sherokee had no prejudices about same-sex dating. Race, religion, gender—none of it was as important as what was inside of someone's heart, her mama had taught her. She was just one of thousands of young people who experiment sexually because of curiosity, the need for love, or perhaps they are questioning their own sexual orientation. Maybe she felt it was safe and not seen as "sex," because one of Rita's steadfast rules was "no sex until marriage."

"I don't know what I am," she confessed to a family member. "Maybe I'm bi, or gay. I don't know."

"Sherokee," she was told gravely, "you know you are not supposed to do that. It says so in the Bible."

"I know..."

Studies of sexual behavior and experimentation reveal children and youth do experiment with sexual behaviors. From playing "doctor" to sneaking looks at salacious magazines, children are naturally curious about the human body. Sexual orientation is not synonymous with these explorations and behaviors. The youth's social circle is believed to have a stronger correlation with same-sex experimentation than actual sexual identity. Girls are more likely to explore sex (kissing, handholding, touching, intimacy) with other girls because of trust, feelings of safety, and security, particularly during between 7 and 12 years of age.[10] Multiple studies reveal the same findings.

Heather did not judge Sherokee nor chastise her for who she dated. She wanted her to be in a happy, safe relationship. She did not care who Sherokee was dating—Hispanic, female, Catholic, Iranian—as long as her daughter was happy and treated right. Heather herself had no prejudices. She felt everyone should be who they were, unless they were hurting someone. She saw same-sex marriage equal to heterosexual marriage, and that people were all equal regardless of skin tone or religion. She was not one to judge others, that she knew was sure.

---

10.   Drotar, Dworkin, Perrin, & Wolraich: *Developmental Behavior Pediatrics: Evidence & Practice* (2008).

In therapy, in the hallways, at meals, and laughing in the day rooms, Sherokee continued to learn new skills to control her anger and work through problems. All was not perfect; she suffered some setbacks. She was written up three times, once for not keeping her room clean, and then she was moved down a level. One of the privileges she lost was being allowed to call home.

Throughout the semester of nine-week sessions, her teachers posted comments:

Semester 1: Sherokee is a very bright young lady. She focuses very hard on her assignments. She is a joy to have in class.

Semester 2: Sherokee loves to participate in class and is very energetic. She is a pleasure to have in class.

Semester 3: Sherokee is a pleasure to have in class. She loves school and is engaging in all activities. She does have her moments where she antagonizes her peers.

Sherokee was still having problems with discussing her traumas. Sometimes she used them in an attempt to garner sympathy. If others felt sad for her, she reasoned, then they would stop asking about it all. *Don't upset her; just let it go. Poor little girl.*

Still, she was managing her behaviors and working on her reactions and anger management. It was hard, particularly when she was mad, but she had to make it work because her discharge date loomed ahead.

CHAPTER 39

The calendar showed March 4, 2013—the date for her exit interview. Sherokee sat smiling and was settled and more mature than the Sherokee who had walked through the Oak Plains doorway in August 2012.

"I feel good," she told the doctor.

"Do you think you're ready to leave?"

"Yes!" This time it was not in defiance or an impulsive thought, but a sincere reply. Sherokee beamed. She was sleeping all night without bad dreams, she no longer heard or saw things that were not there, and her medications seemed to be working well.

The doctor noted Sherokee had not acted aggressive toward herself or anyone else.

She was so proud of herself. She loved the feeling of being in control of her emotions, of being able to express herself correctly.

"Lion level" was the highest a patient could achieve. Despite it being part of her long-term plan, she never reached Lion level. But she was finally released, and she was going to proudly walk out the door next to Gran. She had "reached her baseline of progress with this facility," the report noted.

Others were not so sure. Some of the family believes her treatment "lasted until the insurance gave out. Once there was no more insurance, she was 'cured.'"

Heather and Rita were given detailed, carefully written instructions and advisement on safety plans, triggers and stressors, and supportive recommendations. They were taught the warning signs of suicide and emergency care. A follow-up appointment was made as well as outpatient care with in-home services through American Behavioral Consultants (ABC) in Lebanon, Tennessee.

Finally! Sherokee was gathering her things to be discharged out of Oak Plains. She gave sincere, tight hugs to the staff and to her new friends. The girl that departed the facility, her family agrees, was not the girl who initially walked in. Before, she would have been sweet and loving only sometimes; now it was the norm.

She was now on 7.5 mg of Abilify, 9 mg of melatonin, 50 mg of Trazodone, and a multivitamin. Her discharge diagnoses read:

Axis I (psychological diagnostic categories): PTSD, ODD, Mood Disorder.

Axis II (Personality Disorders): Borderline intellectual functioning.

Axis IV (Psychosocial and environmental factors contributing to the disorder): problems with primary support group, social environment; educational, and legal problems.

Once home from Oak Plains, Sherokee was a much happier girl. She had found that happy medium she had been searching for.

Her medication helped keep her moods level. She still only had a few friends, but they were loyal friends. Sherokee herself was a friend someone could count on, a sounding board, one who gave quick, sincere hugs and said, "I love you!" and meant it. She was aware some of her friends did not get that kind of affection from their family or parents. They relied on one another.

Rita is proud to say that Sherokee was a loyal friend. "If you were her friend, she'd stand up for you through thick and thin," she brags now. She also admired Sherokee's talents. "She was so good at doing art. She was good at doing hair.

Sometimes she would tell me, 'Gran, please let me do your hair for church!'" Rita would go to church with a stylish hairstyle then, bragging to parishioners how her youngest granddaughter had watched a YouTube how-to video only one time and copied it exactly.

Her family loved her new outlook on life. Where once she would attack and argue and fight, she now walked away. Before she left home, she was childish and threw tantrums; now she was using manners and talking things out. She was smiling and laughing. The new medication was helping her to enjoy life, and she was insightful about her mental health. Sherokee was now loving her healthier, happier life.

It did not last.

CHAPTER 40

Rita opened her wallet and sighed heavily. She was missing at least $5, and in this family, $5 could buy much-needed items. Money missing from her purse had become part of life again. If she hid it, it would disappear. If she accused or challenged the culprit, it only escalated the rising tension in the house. But, like everyone else under their roof, she knew who had taken the money.

It was again the norm: Sherokee was stealing money from family.

Rita felt genuine pride in her granddaughter's progress, but was perplexed at her behavior. "Sherokee was a loving child when she wanted to be," she recalls.

From Oak Plains Academy, Sherokee transferred to the sixth grade at Rock Springs Middle School. Sherokee's school was not taking any chances. After perusing her file and history, Rock Springs Middle School officials determined it would be in Sherokee's best interest to be accompanied by an adult as she began the school year. She was placed in a special class, and she was walked from class to class by a faculty member. The adult sat near her in classrooms, casually monitoring the progress. "They automatically deemed her a problem child," Rita fumes.

But Sherokee did not appear to mind that she was kept under close supervision. Sometimes it made her feel special. The students had no idea why she was being watched so closely, and that made it sort of fun, like a secret. Maybe it made her look like a badass, the girl that had to be in a special place for crazies, for mean girls. *Don't fuck with Sherokee Harriman*, maybe they were whispering: *she'll kill you.*

After three months of close monitoring, it was determined that Sherokee was not a threat to herself, to others, or to school safety. The monitoring ended.

At home, the family watched as Sherokee's behavior slowly deteriorated. Sherokee was happy, but it seemed like anything could set her off. She warned other children, "You'd better watch out!" Once she had enough of their bullying and taunts, her reaction was, "I'll kick your ass!"

She scared no one, but that did not stop her from trying.

Often when the school nurse looked up to call her next patient, she saw a pitiful-looking Sherokee Harriman sitting in the chair. The nurse sighed. It was beginning to be a familiar routine in the school's clinic, sometimes after just a few minutes into her first class. "I have a stomach ache," Sherokee would moan to the school nurse. "My head hurts." Sometimes Rita would come to the school to pick her up and take her home.

Testing scores for sixth grade revealed her to be "Below Basic" in Reading/Language Arts, Math, and Science. She scored "Below Proficient" in Social Studies.

Still, Sherokee's report card on May 29, 2013 noted, "Promoted to the 7th grade."

Meanwhile, Sherokee tried to do classwork without listening to the nasty, whispered remarks made by her peers. When the bullying became too much, she went to Gran and Heather, distraught. The adults went to the school and sat down with officials to complain and voice concerns.

"We're looking into it," Rita says she was told.

"We took care of the problem."

Rita filled out two separate "bully reports" and dutifully turned them in. But it felt as if nothing was accomplished. If the bully was hauled in for disciplinary action, classmates labeled Sherokee a "snitch," and things went from bad to worse. Finally she just tired of it all. She stopped turning in bully reports. When Heather would ask for an update, Sherokee would answer with the same reply they got from school officials.

"They're looking into it."

"They took care of the problem."

Her seventh-grade achievement form for the 2013–2014 school year shows "Basic" in reading/arts and math, "Below Basic" in science, and social studies remained "Below Proficient."

Despite the problems in school, there were fun times, good times where everyone in the household was happy together. Sherokee celebrated her thirteenth birthday with Heather, who threw her a party at Lanes, Trains, and Automobiles, a huge facility in nearby Murfreesboro that features a bowling alley, laser tag, video games, bumper cars, and fast food.

Samantha recalls that only a few kids from school attended the party. The majority of party guests were, as always, family members.

As Samantha walked in, she saw Timothy Ashbury, a friend of Sherokee's cousin Matt. She says she spoke with him, asking him why he was there, as Timothy was eighteen and certainly not a school friend.

"Well, me and Sherokee are dating," he reportedly told her.

Samantha thought this both strange and unacceptable: why was an eighteen-year-old man "dating" a seventh-grade girl? And why would anyone allow it? She shrugged it off; it was not the time to voice her opinion—*as if it mattered, anyway*, she silently told herself.

Several of the guests now say they do not recall Timothy being at the party.

The following year, there was her fourteenth birthday party at Sherokee's home where Timothy Ashbury was also allegedly present. There was pizza and cake, and

Heather took pictures of her daughter holding up gifts and smiling widely. Timothy reports the girls rubbed balloons on his spikey hair and giggled. Yet neither Rita nor Heather remembers Timothy being at either party. Timothy dutifully reports he attended both parties.

Timothy says he initially met Sherokee online. He was convinced she was older, around 17 years old, and that was the age she gave him. And so Sherokee began a relationship of sorts with Ashbury. "Sherokee and I had a low-profile and secretive friendship and half relationship," Timothy would say later. "She was interested in a guy who is humorous, responsible, handsome, respectful, and a number of other things." He felt he fit this profile perfectly.

Some people now say Sherokee "dated" Timothy. Others claim they were "just friends." Sherokee would introduce him to her parents. He was a musician, she excitedly told them. He was 18 years old, and she liked that he was older. It made her feel more grown-up to date someone older than the boys in her grade.

Perhaps it was Timothy she had in mind when Sherokee began writing a song:

Boy why won't you date me? I know you said it's cuz of my

age but I wanna know if you think I'm ugly. If you do, I think

I'm pretty. I need to know if you think I'm weak and I need

to know if you think I'm not worth a try...... a tryyy

Timothy would later say he had no idea how old Sherokee was. He states that Sherokee told him she was older, and he believed it, judging by her physical build and her maturity. "I swear, I did not know she was only 13," he says. Despite his attending her birthday parties where age might have been brought up, "It's not like I counted the candles on her cake," he said.

One of Sherokee's family members denies this. "He knew how old Sherokee was. She told him."

A friend of Timothy's was also blunt. "That was a lie. He knew how old she was." Later, this point would become a serious legal issue, not just a debate among friends and family.

CHAPTER 41

In 2013, Heather's ex-boyfriend Mack Edwards was living in Ohio when life took another drastic turn. A cousin asked him a single question:

"Did you know you had a daughter?"

Mack thought it was a joke until he learned the details: Heather had given birth to his child in 2000 and had been raising her in the Nashville area. He found Heather's phone number right away and phoned her. He asked if he did indeed have a daughter.

"It's true," Heather answered. "Do you want to talk with her, if she wants to talk?"

Thus he began corresponding with his daughter, Sherokee Rose, in November 2013. First, they sent one another messages through Facebook. They exchanged photographs. When they both felt it was right, Mack began calling Sherokee that following January. Heather "was glad we were talking," he recalls now. "She didn't have a problem with us talking at all." He adored Sherokee: "She was sweet. Happy. She was a beautiful little girl." He called or texted her daily to check in on her, or just to chat, always complimenting her and supporting her. They exchanged letters and pictures.

Mack continued to follow a now-familiar pattern of arrests, jail, and prison time. He would call Sherokee from behind bars to continue their correspondence, and they wrote letters to one another. He cherished her letters and drawings.

Mack knew Sherokee had a sister, and they talked about Shy. Sometimes Sherokee would confide in him about being lonely, wanting to be popular and pretty. Mack assured her she was beautiful. She was only thirteen, he told her. Life would have much to offer her later down the road.

CHAPTER 42

When visiting her Aunt Samantha and Uncle Jason, Sherokee always ran up to their porch in excitement, She was excited because it also meant spending time with her cousins, including teenaged Matt.

Samantha's first marriage had not been a good one. After divorce and living as a single mom for some time, Samantha met Jason. Jason shared her family values and love of life: religion and family were of utmost importance to him. He would hug Samantha even when she seemed so unemotional, a product of her upbringing she fought hard to change: keep your feelings hidden. Never cry. Jason was so patient with her. Jason loved her kids, her family. He loved Sherokee, too, always calling after her when she left their house, "Love you!"

Yet Samantha and Jason became alarmed when they learned about something Sherokee had said.

"Jason is hot," she said of her uncle who was old enough to be her grandfather. Maybe she was just being a kid. Maybe she was showing off. But it was extremely unnerving.

And then there was the situation with Matt. Sherokee was close to Matt, family members confirm. Matt was sweet and kind, and Sherokee felt safe around him. Matt was never threatening or mean. He did not date much, and he was considering becoming a pastor. "I know he knew nothing about girls," his mother laughs now. "He would come and ask me about girls, body parts and stuff, and I'd have to tell him, 'you need to be having this talk with your daddy.'"

It seemed like every time Matt would visit the Harriman home, Sherokee wanted to be close to him. Too close, in Matt's opinion. She wanted to sit snuggled up to him, hold his hand, give him pecks on the cheek. The time she crawled up in his lap, he stood up quickly to let her fall down so she landed on the floor with a thud. Matt finally had to tell his mother, his face turning red. "Mama, I don't like going over there and her doing that."

He told his mother about one night when he was sleeping over at the Harriman's, and Sherokee had crawled into bed with him. Matt had jumped up, tossing covers and tripping over the blankets to get away. He ordered her to never do it again and to go back to her own bed.

Sherokee might not have understand her actions were inappropriate. Perhaps her boundaries were skewed, and she just was not emotionally mature enough to understand what she was doing or how she was being perceived. One family member wonders if Sherokee just wanted to be close to someone that made her feel safe, and her actions were that of a harmless little girl.

"She's confusing sex with love," Samantha told herself grimly, "just like Heather did." Aloud she told Matt he was not to visit the house unless his parents were with him. Sherokee just did not have the emotional skills or maturity to understand she was acting inappropriately. It angered Matt's mother because she felt no one bothered to correct her.

Matt had grown from a goofy, fun-loving little boy to a handsome seventeen-year-old, a shy young man who loved his family, always putting them first. Both girls and guys counted him as a true friend who would always be there for them.

On September 2, 2013, Matt was spending time at the lake with friends during a Labor Day get-together. At one point he dove into the water, but never came up. It was several hours before his limp body could be untangled from the reeds in the lake bottom and pulled to the surface. His mother held his cold, still hand in the hospital as long as the hospital would allow.

At the time of his death, Matt's plans had been to join the National Guard, then start his own business, "So I can take care of my mom," he told everyone. He discussed being a preacher to share his faith. Everyone knew his most important goal was to take care of his mother as he moved through life. Now he was gone.

There was a vigil, then there were formal funeral services for Matt. It was at the formal services where a girl named Taylor Geffre began talking to Sherokee. Taylor was Matt's friend; the two girls shared their grief.

Taylor liked Sherokee. She found the younger girl to be sweet and shy. Taylor discovered the pretty, blonde-haired girl did not have many friends. "I know how that feels," she admitted to Sherokee. They talked online when on Facebook, and Taylor would read Sherokee's Facebook updates.

She knew Sherokee was being bullied at school, and they talked about it via private message, typing messages back and forth in real time. "I think moms should discipline bullies," Taylor typed into the message box. "Schools need stricter policies about bullying." One theme seemed to run constant with Sherokee. She wanted a boyfriend, someone special who would treat her right; but, she always seemed to attract boys who would treat her bad and then break it off, leaving her heartbroken.

Matt's sudden, unexpected death at such a young age made an impact on Mike and Heather, who realized the fleeting fragility of life. They were married by a justice of the peace on October 18, 2013. It was Mike's first marriage, and in fun he wore a tuxedo-front T-shirt. "I want to wear camouflage," Heather told Mike, "in memory of my daddy." They had a small wedding reception at home. Shy and Sherokee were so happy that they raced through the house screaming. They adored Mike and finally had a real daddy, one who would take them places and encourage them, and best of all, assure the girls he loved them.

The family did have laughter and happiness. They dressed up for Halloween and went to carnivals. At Christmas, despite a tight budget, there were always gifts. Mike had everyone bundle up to tour the Opryland Hotel grounds to see the annual Christmas lights display. They took pictures under the two million lights that decorated trees, fountains, and walkways, turning the hotel entrance area into a spectacular, magical display.

But real life was always lurking. "I hate you!" Sherokee would rage. "I hate you! I hate my life!" Her screaming turned high pitched. "Nobody loves me!" And she burst into tears, her face red. The tantrum was that of a two-year-old, and Sherokee was nearly a teenager.

It was a familiar scene. She was tired of her sister getting all of the attention. She was sick of Shyloe getting on her nerves. She did not understand how her parents could have just thrown her away. The mixed-up chemicals in her body caused her moods to skyrocket and become uncontrollable. She was angry, hurt, and miserable, but not mature enough to understand why life was this way. "I'm going to kill myself!" she would threaten. Later, after cooling off, she would give tight hugs and say, "I love you. I'm sorry."

She was smoking cigarettes and drinking alcohol obtained from the liquor cabinets of her friend's parents. Perhaps this was an attempt to fit in, to be cool and act mature. Or like many people, Sherokee could have been using alcohol to numb the pain and self-medicate.

She could be a funny, sweet, and loyal friend. The problem was, she tried *too* hard to be friends. In a desperate attempt to make friends, Sherokee would "push herself into a group of kids where she didn't belong," Abigail Frazier, Heather's childhood friend, remembers. Abigail's little girl, April, was the same age as Sherokee, and it only seemed natural they would play together just as their mothers had done. By now Abigail was completing a degree in the medical field. She kept a close eye on April, trying to help her steer clear of trouble. She also tried to help Sherokee.

"It seemed like Sherokee needed others to validate her," Abigail explains. "She wanted boyfriends, she wanted to be one of the 'cool' kids. She always wanted a boyfriend."

"Sherokee was boy crazy," her friends will readily agree.

"She would play Heather," recalls a family member. "She had learned she could play Heather, who would try to buy Sherokee anything she wanted, out of guilt. It was a survival tactic, really. Sherokee learned to use people to get what she wanted from an early age."

Rita says, "Sherokee had very low self esteem."

"She grew up hard," one of Heather's siblings adds. "Just like we did."

CHAPTER 43

Katie Nichols took her seat in the classroom, trying not to show how nervous she was, folding her slender, delicate hands over one another to keep them from shaking. It was late August 2014, the first day of school at Rock Springs Middle School.

Katie had been home-schooled until she had been moved to Rock Springs for just a few days until she was bounced back to another school, only to return to Rock Springs on this day. Still, she had not attended Rock Springs long enough to really know anyone, not like the giggling, shouting kids who now sat around her, who all seemed to belong.

It was tough being the new kid. It was more difficult to go from homeschooling to a public school, and the school system had kept her back two grades, so the students around her were at least two years younger. Katie had a slight speech impediment that invited hateful comments from mean kids. Katie was also tiny: at barely ninety pounds and under five feet tall, she could be the brunt of name calling by kids who took her small size and shy demeanor to be weaknesses.

For lack of something to do, she wrote the name of the class neatly across the top of her paper: TEEN LIVING. Nervously, she began doodling on the paper. The heavy classroom door closed and the teacher began to call role as everyone settled into their seats.

And then the teacher called out," Sherokee Harriman?"
"Here."

Katie looked up from her doodling and saw the blonde girl across the room. Katie has an excellent memory for numbers; she recalls the days and classes she took the last time she was in Rock Springs. Sherokee was one of the kids she talked to during her first brief visit at Rock Springs, and she liked her right away.

Later, Katie sought her out. Sherokee remembered her. A friendship blossomed, and the girls became one another's touchstones. It was the type of friendship that withstood many tests, highs to lows, between a lot of giggling and sharing secrets, tears and words of encouragement.

Soon Katie was spending close to every weekend at Sherokee's house. The Harrimans became a second family. As the girls became closer, Katie recalls how Sherokee shared that her "daddy" was in prison, and her "daddy-daddy" was married to her mom. She mentioned her stays in the hospital for her bipolar disease. Katie never judged. Having been diagnosed with anxiety disorder herself, Katie was well-schooled in mental health issues.

Katie got to know Sherokee like a soul mate, and Sherokee confided so much in her best friend. One thing Katie knew for sure: Sherokee always wanted a boyfriend. "She just wanted to be loved," she says now. "To be truly loved by someone." Sherokee seemed to think the school crushes and "dating" should turn into forever relationships: when you had a boyfriend, he would be your boyfriend forever. So when her heart was inevitably broken, it was Katie's shoulder that grew wet from Sherokee's tears. "Sherokee," Katie would say, exasperated. "These people— you might not even know them in two years, five years, ten years from now!"

"But—but—I loved him!" Sometimes Sherokee scared Katie, because she would cry so hard it would cause her to hyperventilate. "I—I—I do!"

One of the boys who caused Sherokee to cry was classmate Alec Seether, who Katie also knew from school.

One day Sherokee posted on Facebook that he was her boyfriend and she loved him *very* much. Weeks later, she posted he was "a little bitch."

"Oh!" she would boo-hoo, "I just—I wish I could just *disappear*!"

"I know how that feels," Katie would commiserate. "Sometimes I just pull a blanket over my head just to feel alone."

On May 6, 2014, Sherokee posted on Facebook:

Maybe if u would listen to me for once, then maybe i would be happy for once.. Calling me out. Pushing me around.. I tried to listen to u but all u do is take over my life and control it. I have a life. U have a life. My life is mine and urs is ur own. I cant deal with all this anymore. I want to give up..

Other times Katie and Sherokee would gossip about school, which Sherokee still hated. Katie, wise beyond her years, loved math. It was so concrete, not like history in which students had to memorize dates first and actual events as an afterthought. Katie watched her best friend struggle through classes. "She just doesn't seem to understand stuff," Katie told friends. "She just has a hard time. I see her grades just go up to down, up to down."

Sherokee discussed her medication for bipolar disorder. Katie, a product of the foster care system and now happily living with her twin brother and family members, wanted to be a psychologist, so she never judged her best friend. She loved what she called "heart-to-heart" talks, discussing rationale, thought processes, reasoning, and looking for answers to complex human behavior. Sherokee did not like talking about her feelings or anyone else's. So instead of exploring her behavior and the root of her problems, she would do Katie's nails and her hair, working on various styles, her fingers slipping through Katie's long, strawberry-blonde hair to produce a five-strand braid or curls and ribbons that spilled between Katie's thin shoulders.

In Sherokee's jumbled world where she never felt she belonged, Katie helped her puzzle it back together. And, Katie says now, "She did some awesome styles on my hair."

As she could be with her family, Sherokee was sweet and loving with friends and boyfriends, but then she could also show her temper. Boys always seemed to let her down, one of her closest friends recalls, and Sherokee wore her heart on her sleeve. Heather knew Sherokee was a loving girl, but Heather felt her youngest daughter was just so afraid to show it. "She has a humongous heart," she would tell others. "It's just every time she gets close to someone, they hurt her."

Mike echoed the sentiment. He found his girl to be sensitive, artistic, and talented when she put pencil to paper. Sherokee loved to draw, and her work was always symmetrical, with clean lines and shadows in the right places. He would see her sitting out on the porch, ear buds stuck in both ears, listening to her favorite music, head bobbing slightly to the beat. He saw the little girl's poor self-esteem, and he felt for her. Trying to make it all better just never seemed to take hold.

"She was a lot like her mom: defiant, hard-headed, and angry," recalls a family member. But Sherokee was, like Heather, honest and loving in her soul. She was growing up a beautiful girl, with soft blonde hair and sparkling eyes. Her skin was soft, with a peaches-and-cream complexion; she did not fight acne like so many young teens. She had a sweet smile, and she was careful with her nails and hair. But it seemed that no matter how hard she tried, there were still taunts in the hallways and lunch rooms.

"Hey fat ass!"

"Ewww, here comes stinky!"

"Show off them big titties, you ho!"

Bursts of giggles. Guffaws from the other kids.

Behind her back, loud enough to hear: "Take a bath!"

Sherokee would lift her chin, tucking a blonde strand of hair behind her ear. She pretended it did not hurt, their words and sniggers. But when it got too much, she would lash back. Her face would turn red, and it looked like she was going to pass out.

This is one reason why it was so much fun to tease Sherokee Harriman. Because when she blew up, it was quite a show.

CHAPTER 44

Sherokee was spending the night with April, whose mom, Abigail, noticed Sherokee was spending more time texting on her cell phone than visiting with April. "Who are you doing all that talking to?" she asked Sherokee, reaching for the phone.

Sherokee was texting with a boy.

But do you like me, she had repeatedly asked him. *Do you think I'm pretty.*

"Why do you need a boy to tell you?" Abigail asked her gently. "You're a beautiful girl. You can do so much in life on your own, don't you know that?"

"I don't know," Sherokee shrugged her shoulders.

"Why do you think you need a boyfriend so bad?" Abigail tried again.

"I don't know."

"Well, why do you need some boy to tell you that you're pretty?"

"I don't know." Another shrug.

Abigail kept an eye on all of April's social networking, and this meant she also could see Sherokee's Facebook and Twitter posts. It just seemed to be a common thread in the girl's life.

Do you like me.
Do you think I'm pretty.
No one likes me.
I hate my life.

Another night, when Sherokee was spending the weekend at April's house, Abigail was flabbergasted by something else. The girls giggled and whispered secrets, listened to music, and laughed. They talked about growing up and what they wanted to do. Just girls being girls.

Then sometime during the evening, Sherokee began talking about how she did not want to live. She wanted to die. She wanted to commit suicide.

It scared Abigail. Abigail knew if she asked her daughter about Sherokee, April would just be vague because she knew her mom would tell Heather, and April was not about to snitch out her buddy.

"I'm going to commit suicide," Sherokee told them. Abigail tried to talk to her, but Sherokee repeated that she hated her life and knew no one loved her.

"Oh, she says it a lot," April later told her mother casually. "It's like an ongoing thing."

Abigail wondered if Sherokee was just trying to get attention.

A telephone call to Heather verified this was a common threat when Sherokee was not getting her way, or felt her parents were being unjust, or her grandparents would not let her do what she wanted. It was, Heather assured her oldest friend, a common ruse to seek attention. It could be the depressive state of a bipolar. As Abigail hung up the telephone, she ruminated over what to do.

That night Abigail, April, and Sherokee curled up to sleep in the living room. "I was not about to leave her alone, back in the bedroom," Abigail Frazier confides now. "Not after what she was saying."

CHAPTER 45

A close family member confides how Sherokee would try her best to act older than her age, to join the older kids in a desperate attempt for attention and friendship. Even when they made fun of, bullied, or refused to acknowledge her, she kept trying. When the kids made it clear she was unwelcome, Sherokee would just try again.

And then there would be more tantrums, when she swung to the other end of the age range and behaved like a toddler. Again the common themes would emerge:

No one likes me.
I hate my life.

Sometimes family members would wonder if Sherokee's self-deprecating remarks were a plea for attention. Was she using the negative words the same way she sometimes used the threats of suicide: trying to get noticed, or because bad attention was better than none? Or should they really believe her threats? Only Sherokee knew that answer; maybe she understood the dynamic. But maybe not.

At home, she continued to fight with her sister. Sherokee and Shyloe would scream at one another, accusing and cursing. Sherokee would swing at her; Shyloe would pick up whatever was handy and hurl it at her sister. Again and again, Heather was forced to separate them, even if she could not be home. She would text Sherokee to stay in Heather's bedroom after school so she would not be near Shyloe.

Yet if an outsider were to treat one of the sisters unjustly, the other would be there immediately to defend her sister. And after a big blow-up, they would make up with hugs and say, "I love you!"

Amidst all of the hard times, there were moments of real tenderness. Heather recalls that one of the times they really did have fun together was when Sherokee would style her sister's hair and put makeup on her.

"Shy, let me put makeup on you," Sherokee would ask.

"No, Sissy!"

"Oh, come on," Sherokee begged. "I saw this makeup trick on YouTube. You'll look pretty!"

Shyloe would usually oblige. When Sherokee finally let her look into the mirror, Shyloe would wonder at her reflection. She did look different—yes, even pretty.

"I told you!" Sherokee crowed. She hugged her sister. "I love you, Shy."

"I love you too, Sissy" Shyloe answered, hugging back.

In moments like this, perhaps the adults in Sherokee's life could believe that everything was normal, and that the girl was just going through difficult teenage years, like many people do. At the very least, such glimpses of the sunshiny little girl she used to be had to be a solace.

CHAPTER 46

Mack Edwards admits, "I'm an alcoholic. And I liked to smoke pot." Mack's wild living caught up with him, and again he found himself donning an orange jumpsuit and being booked into the county jail in August of 2014. (He asked that the exact reason for his incarceration not be shared). He kept up with the news at home, and he stayed in touch with Sherokee, being forthright with her about going to prison. They exchanged letters. When he could, Mack would use the state prison's phone system to place collect calls to Sherokee's home, and he would talk with his daughter.

His release date was slated for September 11, 2015. "There are times when I wish things would've been different," he confides now. "But..." he takes a deep breath "...life goes on. I guess."

Meanwhile, Sherokee penned in her notebook on September 1, 2015:

Day 1 of 11 days until my daddy gets out of jail

She was so, so excited.

On September 3, 2015, they spoke on the telephone when Mack put in a collect call to LaVergne, Tennessee. Mack told Sherokee, "I want to ask you something, but you have to ask your mama first."

"Okay," Sherokee told him.

"How would you like to come up to Ohio and spend the summer with me?"

Sherokee was ecstatic. "Can I?" she squealed. "Really?"

"Yes. But first, we have to okay it with your mama."

She could barely stop babbling. "Okay! I will! I can come meet you? Really?"

Heather and Mike discussed Sherokee going to visit her biological father. Both agreed, because of Mack's history, one or both of them would accompany her to visit for a one- or two-week visit. They did not want to deny their child a relationship with her biological father, but they were acutely aware of Mack's past life.

When Mack and Sherokee each hung up the telephone, both were smiling, laughing even, from excitement. It made his time behind bars bearable, looking forward to a happier future.

Using colored pencils and white handkerchiefs purchased in the commissary as canvases, prison artists can create art. Inmates often send these handkerchiefs home to family and friends. Mack made an agreement with one such artist to draw a perfect image of Mickey Mouse on a handkerchief. Mack mailed it to Sherokee, who proudly posed with the gift for a picture, adding this image on her Facebook wall.

She was growing up so quickly, it seemed. She was becoming a shapely young lady, soon to lose that "little girl" look. It was time, Sherokee decided, to apply for a job.

Mike had promised to take Sherokee to a few local stores so she could put in applications for a part-time job. She dressed for the part in a pretty but simple black-and-white dress, looking older than her years but still youthful. Mike snapped photos of her at the job kiosk as she typed in her information for the electronic application. He posted the pictures on Facebook with pride.

For September 3, 2015, all Sherokee posted on Facebook was:

Can't wait to get a job and be able to get my wants and needs and pretty stuff

But only two days later she followed with:

my life is worthless

BULLYING

Why do people hate me
sooooooooooooooooooooooooooooo much
—Facebook post by Sherokee Harriman, September 1, 2013

CHAPTER 47

The U.S. Department of Health and Human Services defines "bullying" as "unwanted, aggressive behavior among school-aged children that involves a real or perceived power imbalance. The behavior is repeated, or has the potential to be repeated ... include[ing] actions such as threats, spreading rumors, physical or verbal attacks, or excluding someone from a group on purpose."

This clinical definition did not matter to Sherokee Harriman, who instead knew bullying on a much more personal level: being called names, being punched or shoved, or enduring never-ending teasing. "Kids hit her and stuff, just basically being assholes," a close friend says now.

It would make Katie furious, to the point of wanting to attack the mean kids. Katie, an intelligent, good-natured girl, turned furiously defensive when it came to Sherokee.

Sherokee was not constantly being bullied, but there were enough times to make life miserable. Sometimes it was physical abuse, as kids will do, but other times it was words that hurt deeply.

"The bullies made fun of her clothes, her hair, and told her she was ugly," a family friend remembers. "Told her she smelled bad. I wonder now... did she just have all that she could take?"

"She wanted nothing more than just wanting a friend," says another family friend.

Meanwhile, kids in school would not let up.

"No one likes you!"

"Eeew! You stink!"

"Ho-bag!"

"What, are you trying to be pretty!"

One girl would look over Sherokee's clothes: the spaghetti straps, the tight shirt. "Slut!"

Balls of paper bounced off her head. Shoves in the hallway, just enough to let her know she was not welcome. Comments under the breath during classes when the teacher could not hear.

It would happen in other places, not just on campus. The taunts and hateful words sometimes started on the school bus in the morning, then take up again in the afternoon on the way home.

"Take a bath!"

"Look, she's trying to be pretty!"

"You got some big titties, slut!"

The giggles, then guffaws, and she was alone again.

Sherokee just did not understand. She wanted to be pretty, to be popular. "I'm ugly and fat," she would tell her reflection in the mirror, examining her reflection in an attempt to see exactly what was causing the hateful words. She spent hours working on her hair, her makeup, her nails. Sometimes she fought back and stood up for herself.

"It seemed there was no one to push her out of the slump," says a life-long family friend. "She had way too much on her shoulders."

"She had a hard life," one of Sherokee's few friends recalls now.

CHAPTER 48

Heather was always desperately trying to make up for the lost time with her girls. She had a wonderful man in Mike, and she was finally in a good place with support and unconditional love. She continued to feel horrible for having lost the girls and for being a part of their strife. She knew Sherokee wanted to be like other kids and desperately wanted to fit in. So Heather let Sherokee use her old cell phone, and Heather purchased another one. She tried to ensure Sherokee had fun, the fun Heather had always wished for as a child.

One of the things she allowed was for Sherokee to host sleepovers, and one of Sherokee's friends, Angel Hollenbeck, was a regular attendee. Angel admits she was an immature 18-year-old at the time, and Sherokee was 13; they played on the computer and on their cell phones. They giggled and sang along to the radio. Sherokee's musical taste ran mostly in the pop rock genre, and Angel was always wrinkling her nose and making a face at her best friend's favorite songs. Still, they would take turns making up dance step to songs they loved. "Sherokee loved to dance," Angel remembers. Sherokee would videotape herself dancing and singing, using the camera on the family computer. She created an account on YouTube where she would post her videos.

Sometimes they would stroll around their neighborhood, talking about everything from boys—Sherokee's favorite subject—to home life. They shared secrets about their sadness. Angel had met Sherokee during a difficult time:

Sherokee's late cousin Matt was Angel's good friend. They would mourn him together and talk about his attributes. Sherokee drew several pictures in his memory and wrote poems about missing him.

Sometimes Sherokee would confide in Angel how unhappy she was at home. "When I get mad or sad," she sighed, "I just go outside and listen to music." Angel recalls now, "She never mentioned being bullied [to me]. Ever."

Once Angel shared that she had a friend named Nikko who was a practicing Wiccan. Sherokee told Angel she was interested in the Wiccan religion. While she did believe in God, she was also intrigued by other religions, faiths, and ways to worship. She asked Angel all sorts of questions about Wicca. Sherokee told Angel she wanted to meet Nikko and learn more.

"Sherokee wasn't a practicing Wiccan, and she didn't really know much about it," Nikko explained later. "It was more like an interesting thing, something to learn about, for her." Later, there would be a rumor that Sherokee was going to Mankin Park to practice white witchcraft. Angel believes this rumor is unfounded.

As with all of her friends, Sherokee loved to style Angel's hair, do her makeup, and paint her nails. Angel was getting married in 2016. "It's only three years away," she told her friend. "So you can do my hair and nails for my wedding!"

"Yesss!" Sherokee was so excited. They talked about the wedding plans, looking over dozens of dresses, tuxedos, color schemes, and cake decorations in magazines and on line. "Ooh, I love this!" they took turns exclaiming. Angel would fold the magazine pages down to mark them for future reference, to share with Sherokee.

"I saw this new hairstyle on YouTube," Sherokee would say, and that was always followed by her grabbing a hairbrush and some hairpins, forcing Angel into a chair.

Sometimes Katie would come over. She would videotape Sherokee and Angel dancing and singing along to their favorite songs. Sherokee was very good when it came to creating dance routines.

"We always had a blast," Angel says.

It was not so much fun when Sherokee fought with her sister. It could get ugly, Angel says, with shouting and name-calling. Or it could be uncomfortable, with both sisters pretending the other did not exist. Angel observed how Sherokee would resort to shoving and punching. She sat back and watched Shyloe throw things.

"Why don't you get along?" Angel finally asked.

"Something that happened a long time ago," Sherokee responded.

"She was," Angel says now in between wiping tears, "an awesome person to hang out with. She was kind. She loved to sing and dance."

Eventually, Sherokee and Angel parted ways. Angel blames it, in part, on Facebook posts and online arguing between Angel's fiancé and Sherokee. A close friend blames their breakup on Angel's promise to make Sherokee part of her wedding, then dropping that plan altogether. Perhaps this is why Sherokee wrote in August:

i hate when i have these SUPPOSED to be BEST FRIENDS and they dont invite u to hang out or go to a party of some sort and then they use a lame excuse of me not talking to them in a long while but u know what it doesnt matter how much we talk cuz there r ppl who r best friends and go a YEAR without talking to each other and then talk to each other..... but i think those kind of excuses r not worth losing someone who tries to calm u down and keeps u from getting in trouble.....

Sherokee was wounded again when she realized she would not even be a bridesmaid. She would call Angel, listen as Angel talked nonstop about her wedding, then hang up, dejected.

"I really hoped I would be in her wedding," she sighed to Heather.

Heather's heart ached for her daughter, and she would tell her what she always told her: Sherokee was a better person than whoever hurt her. She was loving and kind, pretty and smart. People were just jealous. Then Heather would give her youngest daughter a long, tight hug. "I love you, baby girl."

"I love you too, mama." Sherokee always hugged back.

CHAPTER 49

Sherokee and Taylor Geffre were friends, but not close confidants, and this upsets Taylor to this day. "Maybe she was afraid to share her problems, just like I was. I didn't know then the signs of suicide. I should have. I should have been able to help her." Taylor was glad Sherokee did have a few close friends, like Angel, and Sherokee's best friend Katie.

Taylor sent Sherokee an invitation to Taylor's May 2015 high school graduation party. Sherokee was the first to arrive that night, carrying a wrapped gift and handing it over shyly. She and a friend had pooled their money, and they purchased a beautiful gift set of body wash, soap, and perfume. "Rose and Apple Blossom," Taylor read the label excitedly when she opened her gift. She uncapped the body wash and took a big whiff. "Mmmm!"

"And it's in pink!" Sherokee giggled. "Of course, I had to get something pink—*my* favorite color!"

Despite some recent, sad Facebook posts, Sherokee was "a lot of fun that night," Taylor recalls fondly. The Geffre home had a backyard pool. "The pool was closed, but she begged and begged my mom to open it, so my mom opened it up just for her." Sherokee was a strong swimmer and loved the sport. She felt graceful and beautiful, so weightless and free, gliding through the cool water.

But Rita, who had chaperoned Sherokee, was not pleased. She had told Sherokee that her bathing suit was far too revealing, particularly for a fourteen-year-old girl to be wearing. She did not approve of Sherokee's shorts or what Rita considered to be a revealing blouse. Rita sat back to watch the festivities, her mouth set in a straight line. She just did not like Sherokee's choice of clothing.

Timothy Ashbury and Taylor had both been good friends with Sherokee's deceased cousin Matt, so out of politeness, Taylor had also invited Timothy to the party. Timothy was a musician: he played guitar and dreamed of being a star. Taylor remembers Timothy asking her if he could play some of his music at the get-together.

"I don't think so," Taylor tried to be polite.

"Oh, come on!" Timothy begged. He told her how he has a huge fan base and record companies that were interested in his music.

"No, but thank you," Taylor replied.

Each time she saw him that night, Taylor says now, he was begging to play some of his music. Finally, she relented. "It wasn't very good," she grimaces.

Timothy did receive reviews, but not for his music. Some of his peers thought him to be socially awkward. Others laughed at how he bragged of having famous friends. He lived with his foster parents in one of the better parts of town, in a huge, fancy home—at least, that's what he was telling everyone. He was either attention-seeking, or was a habitual liar, or he really did have the horrible childhood he moaned about. Taylor's mother had an altogether different opinion.

"That boy is dark," Taylor recalls her mother saying. "He has very negative, dark energy."

One of Timothy's best friends would explain later, "Timothy is his own worst enemy. He tries to belong, but he's not accepted. He gets dragged into doing things... things that do him no good."

Timothy made no particular impression on Mike or Heather; he was just a friend who came over to visit with Sherokee. At times he came over, and they left the house to go out. Timothy and Sherokee called one another. They talked in private messages and emails. They texted back and forth.

Those text messages would eventually land him behind bars.

CHAPTER 50

"What are you doing in there!" a teen girl pounded on the locked stall door in the girl's bathroom. "You're taking too long!" She looked back at her friends and they giggled.

"None of your business!" The voice in the locked stall belonged to Sherokee Harriman.

"Hurry up!" another girl shouted.

Another girl referred to the coat Sherokee always wore. "Are you doing something with your ugly-ass coat?"

"The one that looks like a dead dog!" More shrieks about the fake-fur coat of which Sherokee was so proud.

It was so much fun to pick at Sherokee.

Even simple mishaps made her a target, like the time she fell down in the hallway. Instead of offering to help, the kids laughed loudly and pointed at the red-faced girl as she knelt to pick up her scattered books and papers. And the teasing continued for a long time afterward, each taunt a reminder of how she had slipped and landed hard on the cold floor. Stupid Sherokee couldn't even walk!

Addie Sizemore heard what the kids were saying to her friend Sherokee Harriman, and it pissed her off to no end. She knew what it was like to be harassed; at only thirteen years of age, Addie herself had a long history of problems.

Addie had cried to Sherokee about the abusive boyfriend who called her filthy names, who told Addie to go kill herself, and then about his threats to kill Addie. Sherokee was so understanding and kind, but Addie was still miserable and attempted an overdose. She survived, but the medicine permanently scarred her heart .

Addie herself had tried for a long time to be someone she was not. After dating the abusive boy, self-mutilation, drug abuse, and self-loathing, Addie decided to become true to herself. She dyed her hair in rainbow colors that she liked. She dressed how she wanted rather than try to mimic the popular kids. She became open about cutting herself, showing the neat rows of scars along her arms and legs, in an effort to help others. She remembers how, when she was suicidal, Sherokee was a true friend who lent an ear and a shoulder to cry on. You could talk to Sherokee about anything, she said, and she would be there for you.

To Addie, sometimes the overall teasing seemed relentless, and school felt like a battleground. Concentration in the classroom is difficult for kids who become the focus of mean jabs and jokes. It felt like the administration either never tried to help or had no clue of what to do.

In the school hallways, in the lunch room and on the grounds, Addie now listened to the kids who made the cruel comments aimed at Sherokee, about how she didn't fit in and about her clothes. "When she cut her own hair, they laughed at her and said it was too short; they said she looked like a boy." When Sherokee dyed her blonde hair darker, other students "made fun of her, saying they could see her roots." She saw Sherokee was trying to be "preppy," but her financial situation would not allow the expensive, popular, name-brand clothes.

Sherokee was not always the victim: she could dish it out, too. She tried to fight back. She could be mean, her words cutting. She had a temper, and when someone blatantly made fun, Addie saw Sherokee stand up to a few of the bullies. Then Sherokee would hold a grudge against whoever made the nasty remark. Addie sometimes wondered which side of her friend was most real, the mean girl or the sweet girl. Still, Addie recognized the desperation to fit in.

The bullied often becomes the bully, and Sherokee was no exception. In a desperate attempt at combatting hierarchy, or to maybe escape being the persecuted, Sherokee would sometimes bully younger family members.

But Addie knew Sherokee was a sweet girl who was more likely to be your good friend. She knew Sherokee did not really have it in herself to be spiteful. Sherokee was more likely to listen to your problems than to laugh at you for having them. She was often smiling in the school hallways; some of it was real, and sometimes it was a brave front to the barrage of slurs and physical torments.

Addie Sizemore can confirm from personal experience: kids can be mean.

CHAPTER 51

Sherokee giggled, feeling as if she had a huge secret that no one else knew. If anyone found out, they might be shocked. Clutching her cell phone in one hand, she ducked down the hall and into the bathroom, shutting the door behind her and turning the lock softly.

She gave herself a good look in the mirror. As usual, she did not like what she saw: she was fat, stupid, and not at all pretty. At least, that's what some of her fellow students told her. That's what they said on Facebook, on Twitter, in the halls and classrooms at school.

But *he* thought she was something, someone special and pretty. He did not think she was fat, and said she was far from stupid, and he was older and wiser. He had so many plans for the future and seemed destined to be a success. And their conversations were becoming intimate.

She glanced at the door, as if someone passing in the hallway might be able to see through the thin wood, see what she was doing. Tucking a strand of hair behind one ear, she lifted her cell phone to text him.

Now came the secret: she asked him for a nude picture. Then to be safe, she typed in "JK" (just kidding).

With a giggle, she hit send. Her text would travel through cyberspace and land in the phone of that certain young man.

A few moments later, real-time photographs popped up on her cell phone screen. Her mouth dropped open at what she saw.

"I gotta go," she typed in quickly.

She fussed with her hair, looking in the mirror again. She could almost see a pretty girl with good skin, shiny hair, and a pretty smile. The ugly, fat girl that no one liked was overshadowed, if only for a while.

Sherokee Harriman exited the bathroom, casually walking toward her room.

Still, she could not help but smile to herself about this huge secret. She believed if they found out, they just would not understand.

CHAPTER 52

Heather swore she would never call her children names because she bears the emotional scars of growing up in a home where adults cursed at you, name-called and bullied. She would never bully her children, she vowed, never put them down. She wanted so much to break the cycle of violence she had grown up in.

Yet Heather's temper could flare up, particularly when she was not feeling well or when she felt "someone is pushing my buttons," or when Sherokee just continually disobeyed her.

Heather carried two cell phones; one was for work, and the other for personal use. There was one of many days she had told Sherokee not to take her personal cell phone to school, but when she awoke, that phone was gone. She angrily texted her daughter using her work phone:

Your ass is grass! I freaking told you yesterday that I'd need my personal cell phone today N you took it to school anyhow!!!! I don't want any damn excuses!!!!

Sherokee answered in text:

Sorry I thought I asked u to wake me up if u needed the phone today

Heather was livid:

No, I already told you that I would definitely need my phone. You wanted me to wake you up to tell you whether or not that I'll be the 1 waking you up, nothing about the phone.

Sherokee replied in two text messages:

Ohhh
I got it mixed up sorry

The cell phone was a source of many arguments. The following month, another text argument about the phone would fly across the air waves when Heather texted:

You were already told that you had to leave it home. Keep on N I'll make you bring my charger in my room N the phone.

Sherokee:

Wow how rude

It instantly pushed Heather's buttons, as she would say. Her fingers flew across the keyboard:

No, not rude, it's called being a parent N putting my foot down.

Sherokee:

No I think its called being a parent after spoiling their child

This was going too far. Heather shot back:

You're DEFINITELY WAY, WAY TOO DAMN SPOILED FOR YOUR OWN GOOD!!!!

Sherokee replied in two messages:

Well I just wished I wasn't depressed all the freaking time
Maybe then I wouldn't bug and annoy ppl all the time

That next day, Sherokee again "pushed buttons" over a fast-food meal. She texted her mother regarding the food order:

I don't want a plain burger that's gross

After a short exchange, Heather sent two texts:

Then go fuckin hungry
He ordered two plain burgers!!!! Don't like it GO FUCKIN HUNGRY!!!

Sherokee:

Gee thx mother

Heather let her know exactly how she felt:

You're pissing me the fuck off!!!!!!!!!!!!!

Sherokee was either pushing buttons or defending herself when she replied:

No need for cussing I'm getting mad and I'm not cussing at u

Heather responded:

DO NOT TELL ME WTF TO DO!!!!! DO YOU UNDERSTAND ME???? GO AHEAD N FUCKIN CUSS AT ME, I FUCKIN DARE YOU TO!!!!!

Sherokee:

I said I'm getting mad and I'm not cussing at u … Not I'm getting mad and I want to cuss at u

Heather:

But that's an indication that you want to cuss at me!!!! You had better drop your damn attitude!!!!

Sherokee typed:

I don't have an attitude

Heather:

Yes, you do!!!! You're trying to act like you're my fuckin mama!!!!

Sherokee sent one message, paused, and sent another:

No I'm not
I just wish u would stop cussing at me

Heather sent her a final warning:

You had better just stop while you're ahead little girl!!!!! If you correct me in anyway, there'll be EXTREMELY serious repercussions, do you understand me????!!!!

Daddy said that you had better stop ... N he's not fuckin playing!!!!

The argument over the use of the phone would continue into the next day when Heather typed in:

I AM NOT HAPPY WITH YOU, YOU KNEW THAT YOU WERE NOT TO TAKE MY PHONE N YOU IRRITATED YOUR DAD UNTIL HE GAVE IN!!!!!

Sherokee apologized, saying she was not aware she had irritated Mike. Heather was not buying it:

You know damn well, if it's early as hell in the morning it doesn't take much for YOU to get your way!!!!!

Despite Sherokee's claim of innocence, Heather continued:

Whatever, you know exactly what buttons to push N what buttons not to!!!!!

CHAPTER 53

"I can't wait until next year," Sherokee would tell Katie in 2015, "when I can take cosmetology classes!" It was one of the few things she looked forward to regarding school. LaVergne High School had a program for students who were considering work in the cosmetology field. Sherokee definitely planned to be in those classes the next year.

In late April of 2015, Katie and Sherokee both attended a day-long Christian-based camp sponsored by Tennessee's Rutherford County Church. At camp, as usual, both Katie and Sherokee were inseparable, but far from exclusive. Both girls met a handsome, slender, serious young man named Jason Victor.

Jason was intelligent and well-read. Born in Texas, he has lived in several states, finally settling in Missouri. He has no relationship with his parents and lived sporadically with various family members. Despite his unsmiling poses for pictures, he is a romantic at heart and can be quite sensitive. Like many of his peers, Jason favors the Japanese art of anime. He is a firm believer in loyal friendship. He wore his dark hair military short, sporting blue eyes and a rare smile.

When he met Sherokee, he said he liked "almost everything about her. Her personality, her smile. Just her in general. She's a likable person."

Katie, Sherokee, and Jason squeezed together for selfies. Sometimes the girls would snap a photo, catching him off-guard. Sherokee giggled as she tagged his pictures on her Facebook with "my future husband." He told them he was a quiet person, preferring to listen instead of talk. When camp ended, they said their goodbyes, and Jason exchanged contact information with Sherokee. She gave him a nickname: Pandi.

At home, she doodled all over a school binder.

I love my Pandi
My Pandi loves me

They communicated for two months: on Facebook, through texts, and on their cell phones. Jason says now their conversations were so varied he cannot remember everything they discussed. Sherokee seemed to be close to her mom, he recalls. She was jovial, though she admitted she was not always a happy girl. Sometimes she was not in a good mood; he could read this between the lines, or sometimes she would just tell him.

Jason revealed his sad story to Sherokee: he was often suicidal and had attempted suicide several times, each time being brought back to life by medical intervention. He had run away from home numerous times, often going cross-country. He seemed to exist in a perpetual state of sadness.

On May 6, 2015, Sherokee wrote a poem on her Facebook dedicated to Jason:

Dear my loving Pandi,
You keep running from the truth, you know it's true
you think I am crazy for loving you
I wish you could see the angel I see
When you stand in front of me
You think I am your best gift of all
But I wish you could understand, without you I stand 10in. tall
I never believed in the saying "opposites attract"
But the second I met you it became a proven fact

I am cold as ice, while you're hot as fire
As long as I live you're my one and only desire
You're not just my want but also my need
You're like my personal drug, for you I plead
I am the happiest person whenever you're near
But the second you leave I shed a lonely tear

Their friendship waned, then drifted. Their talks became rare. They were still "friends" on Facebook, but they did not text one another as often, and Jason's phone failed to ring with calls from Sherokee. She just did not have the inner strength, nor was she sophisticated enough, to help him in his depression, his anger.

Suicide, running away from home, depression. It was all just a part of their lives. Just things they all had to deal with.

CHAPTER 54

Sherokee dreamed of having a family—a husband and kids—and a career in makeup and hair. She dreamed over wedding cakes and flower arrangements in magazines and on line. She posted some of the pictures on her Facebook, tagging whatever boy she was dating and asking for his opinion on the item. She put much thought into the type of house she wanted. She made a list of "creative baby names."

Girls: Annleigh, Tiffania, Devtonia, Chi Chi, Danyella.
Boys: Charlie, Dawven, Juston, Danni, Danial.

One day as they sat on the front porch of Sherokee's house, Katie and Sherokee began talking about Sherokee's favorite topic: boys and dating.

"Well," Sherokee told her, hesitating. "Sometimes I … kinda … kinda like girls."

Katie was unsure of what her friend meant; she had an idea, but she wanted to make sure. "You mean, *like* like, or like as in *friends*?"

There was one girl, Sherokee told Katie, named Sophia. Sophia went to the same school, and Sherokee found herself attracted to Sophia. But, she explained, she was not sure if she just liked her, or was envious or looked up to her. She just knew she liked Sophia.

Again, Katie did not judge her. She just shrugged and said that was cool; she did not care who you liked as long as they weren't mean to you. It drove her nuts to know

Sherokee could not stand up for herself when she so easily stood up for others.

The subject changed, and they began laughing at how Sherokee was such a morning person when Katie barely managed to drag herself out of bed at the last minute each morning. From there, the conversation turned to cartwheels. It was all so normal, just girls being girls.

Sherokee shared with Katie a seven-page essay on hair and makeup she had completed for one of her classes. In a penciled childish scrawl, Sherokee wrote:

> I might go to college to get to learn more hairstyles ...
> I think I actually want a job being a beautician. I think fashion is my pashian. Because I love styling all kinds of stuff. A beautician to me is just arts and crafts.

And she was always sharing her poems, like one of her favorite pieces she had written for a school project:

> Pink
> It makes me feel tickled
> It's like a seashell
> It is happiness
> Around the world
> Pink
> —"Color Poem" by Sherokee Harriman

Other things made her happy as well. Despite being tone deaf and unsure of herself, Sherokee loved to sing and dance, and she video-recorded herself to share on her YouTube channel for others to watch.

She recorded herself on December 8, 2013, in low light so everything onscreen appears to have been dipped in red, as she sings along with "Fearless."

She videotaped herself sitting on the edge of a bed, strumming a little purple guitar on December 23, 2014, her face blank and expression sad. The video is short, and Sherokee reaches over quick to turn off the recorder.

She sings wistfully into the computer screen on January 4, 2015. Again, the lighting is low and red. One song is about gaining personal power and overcoming the odds. The other is about falling in love, about a handsome man sweeping a girl off her feet.

On June 19, 2015, Sherokee videoed herself dancing. In a purple top and blue jean shorts, she whirls and steps to the music, mouthing the lyrics to pop love songs like Naomi Scott's "She's So Gone," Bridget Mendler's "I'm a Blonde," and Demi Lovato's "Confident."

Later, on January 24, a video shows her standing in the kitchen, wearing black and white, spinning on the linoleum in sock feet, singing along to a song about a girl gaining her strength after being dumped by a boy.

On April 19, Sherokee released another YouTube video. She sings into the computer screen, "Fall to Pieces" by Avril Lavigne. Pushing her long, dark blonde hair away from her face, rolling her eyes, making a sincere effort, enjoying herself. As in all of her videos, her voice soft and sweet.

Always, the same theme: unrequited love, a brave recovery after a tough breakup, gaining personal strength and identity. They were qualities she longed for.

—

Sherokee's eighth-grade academic reports at Rock Springs Middle School show a student whose progress had hit a lull. An undated progress report reports her grades as 71 in language arts/reading, 63 in social studies, 77 in science, and 72.5 for pre-algebra.

Her 2014–2015 eighth-grade report card for the second, third, and fourth, quarters reveals an ongoing academic struggle:

• Her language arts grade roller-coastered, beginning with an F, rising to a C, and dropping to a final grade of D.

- Science stayed a steady C.

- Her best subject, math, plummeted from a D to an F, finally back to a final grade of D.

- Sherokee's old nemesis, social studies, remained an F from the beginning of the second quarter to the fourth quarter.

Her ending grade point average was 72.25, which was barely passing.

Her eighth-grade Tennessee Comprehensive Assessment Program (TCAP) test for the 2014–2015 school year showed Below Basic in reading/language arts, Proficient in math, and Basic in science (there was no social studies score). As an overall numerical score she received a 698 out of a possible 900, which ranked her as Below Basic.

A common plan for a student in this difficult situation would be to develop an Individualized Education Plan. An IEP is a program utilized by many schools to create "an opportunity for teachers, parents, school administrators, related services personnel, and students (when appropriate) to work together to improve educational results for children with disabilities. The IEP is the cornerstone of a quality education for each child with a disability."[11] It is used to assess current performance, goals, and measurements.

There are no IEP records in any of Sherokee's school records. There was no mention of an IEP whatsoever.

Out of the 171 days of school, Sherokee was present for 156 days. Most of her absences were unexcused. There are 16 tardies on her record, half of which were unexcused.

On her final eighth-grade report card, in the top right-hand side of the form, are the words

Promotion Status: Promoted

---

11. U.S. Dept. of Education, A Guide to the Individualized Education Program

CHAPTER 55

To this day, Sherokee's family continues to insist there was no way Sherokee would have ever attempted to stab herself, and to play with knives was so out of character for her. Mike uses an example to verify this belief; he smiles because the incident was so typical of Sherokee.

Mike had pulled up to the local pawn shop with Sherokee in the passenger seat and a friend in the backseat. The girls were playing on their cell phones, giggling and swapping secrets. He exited the car and Sherokee opened the door to join him, cell phone in one hand.

But she lost her footing and hit the pavement. Her phone went flying, and she began screaming in pain. Mike raced around the car to help her. Her shrieks sounded like she was in horrific pain, as if she had broken a bone. He found her sprawled out on her stomach and rolling over when he knelt down.

"What happened!" he asked, heart pounding. "Chicky, are you okay!"

"My knee! My knee!" she howled.

He saw then she had caught her ankle in the seat belt retractor. Helping her sit up, he examined her knee. It was scraped, with a bit of blood, but otherwise she was unhurt.

The cell phone received the worst damage. The screen had spider webbed, and a corner busted off to reveal some of the circuit board. Still, Sherokee was crying, rocking back, clutching her leg. "My knee! My knee! Owwwww....!"

Mike sighed and shook his head, helping her to stand.

Sherokee did not seem to have any tolerance for pain, including emotional wounds. Of all of her friends, her best friend Katie knew this to be true. Sherokee was sobbing on the phone the last time they talked.

Sherokee was convinced her latest boyfriend was her true love that would last forever. She was planning on spending the rest of her life with him when the boy let her know there was no future; he had found a new girl.

Sherokee called Katie that night, sobbing. Katie was in bed, and she burrowed under the covers so her family would not hear her.

"He—he—he d-doesn't love me!" Sherokee squalled.

Again, Katie patiently explained that their current life situations would not last forever; change was always around the corner. "Besides, isn't he, like, eighteen or nineteen? And you're only thirteen!"

Age didn't matter, Sherokee choked back tears, if you really loved someone. And she and her now-ex had something special.

Katie was exhausted, and the repetition of Sherokee finding the love of her life, breaking up, and then crying her heart out was too much to bear this late. She promised Sherokee they would talk later, and she had to go to sleep or she would be in trouble. They spoke a few more minutes, Sherokee mentioning how Shyloe was on her last nerve again, and Katie hung up. She promised herself she would listen patiently next time. Besides, it was nothing new: Shy was always on Sherokee's nerves.

Sherokee not only could not handle pain in the present, she also seemed unable to forget her past wounds. And some seemed worse than others.

Like all of the boys she dated, Sherokee was head over heels in love with Alec Seether, with whom she had a brief relationship back in 2013. She wrote his name all over her binders, and she let the world know via Facebook how she was so crazy about this young man. On September 28, 2013, she posted a picture of Alec with a list:

> I love Alec
> I love him with all my heart
> He is the best thing that has ever happened to me
> I wish I could see him on the weekends
> I wish we could see each other every weekend
> But I think that we see each other enough at school
> So that is all for today

Then everything took a bad turn and the relationship ended on a sour note. Alec would eventually exchange barbs with Sherokee on social media in late December 2014, both name-calling each other: ugly, bitch, whore. She wrote he was "an ugly little bitch."

Angry words, name-calling, exchanging insults on social media: each young person seemed to forget that, not long ago, he had texted her a truly sweet message. He assured Sherokee that he had her back when she faced the bullies and mean kids.

Morning of September 5, 2015:

"My life is worthless"

Going to the park anyone wanna join its mankin park

—Last Facebook post by Sherokee
Harriman, September 5, 2015

CHAPTER 56

September 5, 2015, was like any other Saturday morning in Sherokee's home. Mike and Heather had contract work, so they packed up to go clean a residential home for a new client. They were hoping it would become a regular job. "Can I go?" Sherokee asked.

"No," Mike told her. "Mrs. Hendrick is a new client and might want to hire us to do some more work. It wouldn't look right to have your kid there." So Sherokee stayed at home, a place that also seemed unwelcoming.

"It's like she didn't have anywhere to go," Katie would later explain. "She couldn't go into her bedroom because that was her sister's space. She couldn't go into her Gran's room. Sometimes she got to hang out in her parent's room."

Rita had gone to visit one of her daughters.

At 8:17 a.m., Sherokee posted on her Facebook:

My life is worthless

Sherokee, bored with sitting at home, had much on her mind as she was filtering through her wardrobe. She was not like some of her peers at school who boasted closets stuffed with designer clothes and $200 sneakers. But she was good at coordinating, so she carefully chose the outfit for the day: pink panties, a black bra, and one of her favorite pairs of denim shorts. She slipped on a gray sports bra as the multicolored blouse she selected was too revealing in places.

For fun, she chose two different color socks that offset the colors in her blouse.

Sherokee was slipping a pair of leopard-print sneakers on her feet when she decided to go to Mankin Park to be alone, to do some thinking. The weather was not too hot or cold for a walk. It was balmy outside. The forecast called for rain later that night.

Sherokee was using Heather's personal cell phone, and at 12:03 p.m. she text-messaged Heather:

Can I go to the park?

When she did not receive an immediate answer, she tried again:

Mama?

Heather stopped working for a moment to text her back:

Idk. I don't really trust the male gender in that neighborhood. The only way you can go is if you text me EVERY 5 minutes.

Sherokee:

Umm ok

Heather:

I want to make sure you're ok

Sherokee:

OK

Sherokee had recently dyed and trimmed her hair into a dark bob, and she brushed her hair and studied her face in the mirror, trying to decide if she liked the new look. The hairstyle showed off her pretty eyes; it made her face appear pixyish. Her pink cheeks and pretty skin still made her look younger than 14.

Rita hated the hair color. She also did not appreciate Sherokee dyeing or cutting her hair after Rita's explicit instructions to leave that to professionals. Sherokee, defiant, had dyed it anyway.

Rita had returned home, so Sherokee asked, "Gran, can I go to the park?"

"What does your mom say?"

"She says it's okay."

"Then I guess it's okay," Rita told her. "Just come home for dinner."

"Okay! Thank you."

Slipping into her white jacket, Sherokee stepped out of the house, departing for Mankin Park.

"I'll see you later," she told Rita.

"That's the last time I saw her," Rita says hollowly.

As she walked, Sherokee used the cell phone to check her Facebook page; she noted a friend had responded to her earlier post of "My life is worthless." The friend had responded at 9:43 a.m., adding a sad face and a heart shape to the words:

No its not. I love youuu"

Sherokee responded at 12:09 p.m.:

No it really is.

It was good to go to the little park, to escape and close up into your mind, where you could think clearly and not be interrupted. Maybe it would be a chance to hang out with someone. Maybe make a new friend.

Sherokee again used her cell phone to make a 12:10 p.m. post on Facebook:

Going to the park anyone wanna join its mankin park

And with that she walked down the road, facing traffic, hope peeping out of her heart that someone would be there and they could enjoy one another's company. It was close to noon.

Sherokee had only a few hours to live.

She turned left at the corner onto Mankin. Anyone driving by saw a pretty girl strolling down the street, studying her cell phone, lost in thought.

She took the main entrance into Mankin Park, glanced to her left to see several teens lounging about on one of the four picnic benches under the pavilion. She recognized one girl as Debi, who went to her high school but was not a part of her social circle. Sherokee did not recognize the other girl. There were two boys with the girls. Alec Seether was one of the boys; he sat with his sister Angelique and a younger boy. Donny Duroy sat with the group. They were all texting, talking, and looking up music on their cell phones. Debi seemed to be trying to get a signal on her phone, as she kept holding it at various angles, squinting at the screen.

None of them acknowledged her presence, not even Alec, with whom she once professed to be madly in love.

Staring at the ground, hands shoved into her jacket pockets, Sherokee walked aimlessly about, kicking at the occasional stone. She walked to the back of the park and sank down into a seat on the swing, head down.

Debi says she broke away from the group and approached Sherokee shyly. When she was close enough for her to hear, Debi said by way of greeting, "Hey."

Sherokee looked up at her, then back at the ground, pushing herself in the swing just slightly, using the toe of her leopard-print shoe.

"Are you okay?"

"Yeah." Barely audible.

Debi tried again. "So, how's it going?"

No answer.

Debi stood there, trying vainly to decide what to say. She felt bad that Sherokee seemed so sad, but she just did not know what to do. "Well," she finally said, "see you later."

Still no reply. Debi turned to slowly walk back to the group.

The teens chatted a bit, Allie looking over at Sherokee. She knew Alec used to date Sherokee. Allie was now dating Alec, but lately she felt the relationship slipping away. Finally she told her friends, "I have something to tell that bitch."

"Leave it alone," one of the boys told her. He just wanted to chill with friends today, not be dragged into someone's drama. Allie had a habit of doing that, always starting shit with people who didn't even know her. "Just leave it," he repeated.

The teens returned to their cell phones and their music, talking about school and friends and people they knew. Debi again checked her own cell phone in the hopes she could actually get a signal.

Someone noticed when Sherokee slipped out of the swing and headed back toward the park entrance, head down, her short dark hair hanging like a bell around her face. She looked up briefly to glance down both sides of the street to cross, heading for the stop sign across the road.

"Come on," Allie told her friends. "I need to tell her something."

"Stop it," Donny told her.

"No, it's okay." Allie jumped up from her perch on the bench and headed for the street. "I just want to tell her something."

Debi joined her and together, with the boys behind them, walked toward the entrance of Mankin Park as Sherokee stepped up on the curb to head for home. Angelique and Micky trailed from a distance.

"Hey!" Allie called out at Sherokee, causing the girl to turn around to look at her. Debi, Alec, and Donny relaxed. Okay, she was just going to talk to her.

That was when Allie Trace shouted at Sherokee, "Hey bitch, you're a ho!"

Sherokee's head went back slightly, as if slapped, and her eyes widened at the outburst. Her face read confusion and disbelief.

Debi's jaw dropped in amazement. The boys merely stared.

Unbeknownst to any of them, life was about to change in a big way.

CHAPTER 57

On September 6, 2015, Mack Edwards telephoned his family in Mansfield, Ohio. He was already packing his things neatly into a cardboard box, anticipating September 11 when he would walk out into the free world. Best of all, he was going to spend the summer with his daughter, getting to know one another after meeting in person for the first time.

Mack made a collect call to home to ensure they had plans set for the 11th. "When are ya'll planning on coming to pick me up?" he asked the family member who picked up the phone.

His family had terrible news to share. As he learned about Sherokee's fate, his hand held the telephone in a death grip.

Mack knew he would not be allowed a request to be released early. Any emergency had to be verified by administration.

Mack's sister telephoned prison officials with the horrible news of Sherokee's death. Prison staff are well educated in all of the tricks that inmates try to gain release or any type of benefit. Initially, they were leery of the story told by Mack's sister, thinking it was a hoax. When officials were able to verify the tragic loss of his daughter, Mack was notified.

On the same date Mack Edwards was learning of his daughter's demise, county medical examiner and forensic pathologist Dr. Feng Li was posed over the cold body of a 14-year-old white female for the purpose of conducting the autopsy. Sherokee had been transported from Vanderbilt

University Medical Center, where she was taken off life support. A company called Middle Tennessee Removal Service carried the remains to Nashville's Center for Forensic Medicine Center for examination. Because her death had been initially deemed a suicide, an autopsy was scheduled. It was not the first time Dr. Li had conducting an autopsy of a child, nor would it be the last.

Dr. Li's clinical diagnosis would determine if the death was accidental, suicide, or homicide. He would gather all of the notes and later type out the report, including a pathologic diagnoses, external and internal examinations, and a summary.

Dr. Li noted a stab wound on the left side of the abdomen; the direction of the knife traveled down into the flesh, toward the subject's back, and to the right. The knife injured the stomach, the intestines and mesentery, the abdominal aorta, and the vena cava. The cut had caused "extensive pelvic hemorrhage." There were no other marks on the body or the head.

There was evidence of the medical emergency team's work: the tubes, the EKG pads, and multiple puncture marks. Even the hospital wristband remained on the young victim's arm.

There was no sign of damage indicative of strangling or smothering; there was no pathological sign of hemorrhage, fractures, or damage to the airway. The digestive system showed no sign of internal issues, and the lungs showed the deceased was not a smoker. The subject showed no evidence of pregnancy, no broken bones, no history of heart disease. There was some bile in the gall bladder. Dr. Li would write numerous times, "The ... system is unremarkable ... normal."

Samples of blood, bile, and vitreous humor were removed for toxicology testing. The toxicology reports showed nothing remarkable. The blood test revealed the presence of benzodiazepines, a drug used to treat anxiety.

Midazolam and Alpha-hydroxymidazolam were present from the emergency room injections. The bile and vitreous humor were not tested; testing was not necessary.

"Based upon the circumstances surrounding death, as currently known, the cause of death is stab wound of the abdomen," the final report summary read. "The manner of death is consistent with suicide."

CHAPTER 58

LaVergne Police Department officials had to tread lightly in their treatment of the Sherokee Harriman case. The newspapers and local television news were blaming Sherokee's death on bullying. No one seemed to want to check the story or dig too deeply. A kid committing suicide because she was bullied was sensational. The public was outraged: another child lost to bullying? When would it end? Why weren't police doing something about it?

The story that Sherokee killed herself solely because she was bullied, even without proof, caught like a brushfire, fueled by anger and grief. The case also involved juveniles, so the information was carefully protected. There was little officials could say. This made Sherokee's loved ones even more suspicious.

The investigators gathered all of the evidence: eyewitness testimony, the coroner's report, information gleaned from interviews, and, of course, social media. Social media was a gold mine of information for investigators. Facebook, Twitter, Snapchat, cell phone records, text messages, YouTube; all of it was there for anyone to see.

In mid-September, LaVergne Police Department spokesman John Fesmire announced to the media the department was continuing to investigate the case and no arrests had been made. After they gathered every scrap of evidence available the investigators would turn the case over to the district attorney, who would make the decision to prosecute.

Sherokee's family was demanding an arrest. They told one another and posted on social media that it was only fair that the teens, and at the very least Allie, be arrested for causing Sherokee to commit suicide.

Timothy Ashbury's name came into the mix as well. Reportedly, he had posted on his Facebook page,

Today I made a girl commit suicide[12]

Posts floated across Facebook pages blaming Ashbury for bullying Sherokee literally to death. Bullying and Sherokee's death became synonymous long before the police investigation was near completion.

One of Sherokee's family members began a nonprofit organization, Stand Against Bullying Tennessee (SABTN) in Sherokee's honor. Like the rest of his family, he was convinced bullying drove Sherokee to suicide. One of the goals of SABTN is simply to make bullying illegal.

The Wednesday following her death, LaVergne High School students were asked to wear pink, Sherokee's favorite color, in her honor and as a sign that bullying was not tolerated. There was a pink balloon release from the outside bleachers. While it helped Sherokee's school chums with their grief, the memorial also caused issues. One of Sherokee's friends reports, "During that day, all of these people were running around, saying, 'she was my best friend.' They didn't even know her. Or they had been mean to her." Other students reported the same things. Kids seemed to revel in the ceremony of wearing pink and releasing balloons without truly grasping the meaning.

---

12. The post was reported by various persons. Timothy shut down his Facebook soon after. The post has never been verified.

Sherokee's family members told the media that seeing the alleged bullies across social media, knowing they were going unpunished, added insult to their sorrow. The bullies did not appear to be affected and sure did not seem to care they were party to what the Harrimans considered murder. Sherokee's family kept up with the four teens on Facebook, reading their posts and then commenting on their own Facebook pages. The family remained angry at what they saw as a slow and biased investigation.

The thorough law enforcement investigation into the case ruled out murder or that any of the teens had played a part in physically harming Sherokee that fatal day at Mankin Park. The investigators determined, by legal definition, there was no bullying. Instead it was legally labeled a "fight." The girls had simply fought over a boy, they would explain.

On September 16, LaVergne police chief Mike Walker announced in a press conference the case materials were going to the district attorney, and from there, "the D.A. would be the one to move forward" in charging the teens with any crime.

Walker explained bullying as "a very, very broad term." Because Tennessee does not have a bullying statue, "the closest thing we might have would be maybe harassment."

The Tennessee Code for Criminal Offenses defines Harassment (39-17-308.) as a person who intentionally:

(1) Threatens, by telephone, in writing or by electronic communication, including, but not limited to, text messaging, facsimile transmissions, electronic mail or Internet services, to take action known to be unlawful against any person and by this action knowingly annoys or alarms the recipient;

(2) Places one (1) or more telephone calls anonymously, or at an hour or hours known to be inconvenient to the victim, or in an offensively repetitious manner, or without a legitimate purpose of communication, and by this action knowingly annoys or alarms the recipient;

(3)   Communicates by telephone to another that a relative or other person has been injured, killed or is ill when the communication is known to be false; or

(4)   Communicates with another person by any method described in subdivision (a)(1), without legitimate purpose:

(A)   (i)   With the malicious intent to frighten, intimidate or cause emotional distress; or

(ii)   In a manner the defendant knows, or reasonably should know, would frighten, intimidate or cause emotional distress to a similarly situated person of reasonable sensibilities; and

(B)   As the result of the communication, the person is frightened, intimidated or emotionally distressed.

Harassment is a Class A misdemeanor.

Again, Sherokee's family was aghast. Their child was called filthy names, surrounded by a group of kids and shouted down. How was this not bullying? How is this not harassment? "They called her a ho and a slut! They cussed her out!" Heather raged, tears in her eyes. "How is that not bullying!" None of it seemed fair nor logical.

"I think it was homicide because [the teens] drove her to it," one of Heather's siblings told the media. "They pushed her to the point where she felt she had no option."

Sherokee's family continually asked one another why the kids were not being punished for taking part in Sherokee's suicide. If being called names, threatened, and shouted down was not bullying, just what exactly was bullying, anyway?

CHAPTER 59

The Harriman's financial situation was so dire, they wondered how they would give their child the proper burial she so deserved. Someone suggested an online fundraiser where people could donate money toward expenses, leave messages for the family, and sign a virtual condolences log. They needed $6,000, and through the fundraiser, Heather and Mike were able to raise $4,000. A portion of the donations were also used to make a donation to a nonprofit organization that assists suicidal teens.

A bit of the money was saved back to take Shyloe somewhere the girl had rarely been: to a mall for a shopping spree.

Shyloe tried on a pair of cowgirl boots in a pretty, feminine pink. She strutted around the store, beaming at herself in every mirror she could find. An accompanying adult says now that Shy just glowed. "I've never had new clothes before!" she said, immensely proud of those boots and her new clothes.

Visitation for her sister was held on Thursday, September 17, 2015, from 4 to 8 p.m. at Rutherford County Baptist Church in Smyrna.

At the viewing, "There seemed to be a lot of tension," a family member reports. "I can't explain it. There was just tension. Heather was outside smoking most of the time, which I didn't understand."

Heather did stand outside smoking to ease her own tension and to keep herself from crying. Her history of abuse and the family rule of "no crying, show no emotion" were still ingrained into her.

Katie, sobbing, wondered just how much a heart could ache before it would burst. Little Katie had had a lot of ups and downs in life and was always able to take it in stride. But losing Sherokee was like losing a part of herself.

Shyloe Harriman had not been able to sleep, and if she did sleep it was full of horrific nightmares. It finally sunk in that her Sissy was gone forever. She was not coming back. Sherokee's messy bed was cold at night; the magazine pictures of her favorite singing and acting stars taped to her side of the room would stay the same because Sherokee was not there to add pictures to the collage.

Shy continued to have problems expressing herself and began acting out, screaming at the adults. Formerly an affable and sweet girl, she was turning angry and spiteful. She returned to her old coping skills, hitting herself and banging her head into the walls. She physically lashed out at her grandmother.

Heather and Mike would bunch up thick blankets and pillows to make a spot at the foot of their bed at night, where Shyloe could curl up like a little wounded bird and try to sleep. She would not be able to sleep in her own bed for months.

The funeral was held on September 18, 2015.

The crowd was somber, some already wiping tears, as they walked slowly into the Rutherford County Baptist Church to take a seat in the pews. The sanctuary was nearly filled to capacity as many family members gathered to show their respect and support. They went to Heather, Mike, Rita, and Mack to express tearful condolences and to gaze at the little girl in the casket.

Someone had made buttons with a red frame and red slash across the middle with the word "bullying" in the center. A picture of a beaming Sherokee was featured. People pinned the button to their shirts and blouses.

Mack looked handsome in black pants and a black striped shirt, his hair cropped short. He donned a "Stop Bullying" pin featuring his sweet daughter's image, pinning it carefully over his right chest pocket. Then he walked slowly to the casket, removing his oval-framed eyeglasses to wipe away the constant tears.

It was the first time he saw his daughter in person, and she was lying in her white casket.

Heather wore pink, her daughter's favorite color. She used a handmade ribbon adorned with Sherokee's name to pin back her long hair. Like everyone else, she donned a "Stop Bullying" pin.

Katie, Sherokee's very best friend, wore pink, including a pink bow in her hair. Her pain was visible, etched in her thin, pretty face as she sobbed. Sherokee could not be gone. It was not possible,

Timothy Ashbury was not in attendance. "With all that was going on at the time, I decided it was best not to go," he explains now. He truly liked Heather and Mike, and he was close to Sherokee, but he had other reasons, soon to be revealed, for not attending the funeral.

Sherokee Rose Harriman was laid to rest in a beautiful white casket with rose-gold trim. A huge spray of red roses sat atop the lower portion. Pink roses were embroidered into the upper inside lid; Sherokee lay on a white cushion. She wore a dress that Samantha had purchased for her not so long ago. "She loved that dress," Samantha told others. "At tax time, I would take the girls shopping, and that's when I bought her the dress." Sherokee wore a dark long-sleeved sweater over the dress to cover the marks and bruises left on her arms when the EMT response team and the medical staff fought to save her life.

A teddy bear, its fur covered in pink, white, and red hearts, was tucked under both hands.

Sherokee's dark hair was combed and tucked behind her ears to frame her face; it was the haircut she had given herself and was so proud of. As was her standard, her nails were done to perfection. Mike had crafted multicolored crosses to lay alongside her upper body. All things important to Sherokee—hearts, the color pink, a stuffed animal, pretty nails and hair, and roses—now represented a life cut short.

In death, she appeared older, even stern. Possibly due to the position of her head, her chin bent low. It was enough for someone passing by her casket to recall, "She looked like an old woman laying there." The transformation was shocking.

When he could see through his tears, Mack took a few photographs. It was the only time he was able to take a photograph of his daughter. His family in Ohio, unable to make the journey, had requested that he take photographs so they could "be" at the service, to share in the grief. Mack, unfamiliar with social media, says it was an accident that the photos appeared on his Facebook. It angered Heather's family, who found it morbid. Later, a few family members and friends would discuss the photographs on Facebook, blasting Mack for what seemed like blatant disrespect.

Both Mike and Mack spoke at the services. Mike spoke of the loving little girl who called him "Daddy." Mack told the congregation, "I never got to meet my daughter." Pastor Paul Chisgar spoke of his own life, shared Biblical verses, and waxed philosophic of childhood. He had baptized Sherokee. Now he was laying her to rest.

A family friend sat numb in the pew, the words spoken from the pulpit washing over her, glancing at all of those who came to pay respects. "Sherokee was an angel here on earth," she found herself thinking. "God puts everyone here on earth for a reason. The reason Sherokee was put on earth was to bless so many people's lives."

Sherokee's uncle Jason was hurt and shocked he was not asked to be a pallbearer. He adored Sherokee and always worried about her and her sister. He would tell her "I love you!" when they saw one another, and Sherokee always echoed the sentiment back to him. Tears streaming down his face, he now had the job of pushing her casket out to the pallbearers. It was the last thing he could do for her. His love and grief for her seemed to radiate from his big hands into the casket.

One of the pallbearers who helped carry the casket to the hearse and watched as it was slid into the back of the sleek, black vehicle dropped to his knees, sobbing. He was helped into an awaiting car where he collapsed across the seat. "I have to get it together," he moaned, tears washing his face. He still had to help carry the casket to the grave. "I have to get it together or I can't do this!"

Arriving at the Mapleview Cemetery, the group of mourners gathered around the closed casket. After a few words at graveside, the casket was slowly lowered into the ground.

It is tradition for cemetery groundskeepers to cover the casket once it is lowered into the ground and mourners have departed. But after the graveside service, Mack Edwards stepped forward and grabbed a nearby shovel. He scooped up a pile of the soft, brown earth and dumped it into the hole in the ground.

It made a hollow sound as it landed across the casket. Mack dug in again, and another heavy thud echoed.

It was the last thing he could do for his little girl, to ensure someone who loved her took the final step of laying her to rest. As he shoveled dirt, tears coursed down his face, his eyes red and puffy.

Soon the other men stepped forward to join in the process. They passed the shovel and, one at a time, they scooped freshly-turned earth into the grave.

"SHE DID NOT COMMIT SUICIDE"

im a 13 year old who likes puppies

—Sherokee Harriman twitter account, @sherokee1

I am 13 years old I love typing and boys that treat me right and don't want for 1 thing and only that 1 thing. also I recently had a guy that cheated on me.

—Sherokee Harriman twitter account @chik129

CHAPTER 60

When the district attorney declined to press charges against the kids who were at Mankin Park that day and the case was soon closed in early October 2015, Sherokee's family and friends felt as if they had been cheated.

"It was not bullying or harassment," an investigator tried to explain to Sherokee's family. "It was a fight over a boy."

The family refused to believe it was true or fair. They felt helpless: Sherokee's tormenters were never legally punished, no officials seemed to take bullying seriously, and suicide just did not seem plausible. "They closed the case real quick," Mike and Heather agree. Because of this, Sherokee's parents suspect possible foul play or even police corruption due to the fact one of the bullies' relatives worked in law enforcement. And it just seemed like media interest in Sherokee's story was out like a light once the decision was made.

Yet she left behind so many mourners: family, her few dedicated pals, people who did not even know the sweet-faced girl who sent condolences. "My baby girl's story has reached all the way to Hawaii," Heather announced on her Facebook.

Jason Victor pounded the message into his computer's keyboard with anger:

How many times do I have to say it she did not commit suicide

Jason, at fourteen, was aware of the signs of suicide. He had worked to help friends who were suicidal. He had been the target of bullying himself, and he championed anyone who was being bullied. "I do my best to help people like that," he says.

Although their romance was over, he still thought of Sherokee, the pretty girl he had met only a year before at the Christian-based day camp. Katie and Sherokee had been the highlight of his event.

Sherokee had been Jason's cheerleader, someone who would help him rally when he felt so down. Jason tended to keep his problems to himself, but he found it easy to talk to Sherokee.

Jason tells of a long talk he had with Sherokee, via text, on September 4. Sherokee was her old self, and she mentioned she was upset over what kids were saying to her, but she never indicated she would take her own life. It was the first time he heard she was being harassed by other students. They were physically hurting her, she told him, calling her names.

"Well, they're assholes," Jason told her.

He knew Sherokee was not one to report anything to school officials, preferring to just duck her head and tolerate it all as best she could. He knew she could lash out when pushed too far.

"Well, I'll help you do something about those assholes," Jason promised her before they stopped texting.

The next day, Jason tried to call Sherokee to see how she was doing, to offer advice and lend an ear. Instead of hearing his friend's voice, Heather picked up the phone.

"Her mom answers and drops it on me," he recalls. Heather tearfully explained Sherokee's death.

Jason could not believe it. He could not conceive any of it. Sherokee putting a knife to her body, much less plunging it in, was so improbable. He had no idea what really took place in the park, but he knew in his heart suicide was not even a consideration. Maybe she had the knife just to wave around, which was almost laughable. Even holding a knife to scare someone did not fit her personality.

Rita Harriman does not believe it was suicide, but murder. "I think those kids grabbed her hand and the knife and made her stab herself," she says bluntly. "She hated pain. She hated blood. She had just wrote a letter days before [it happened] writing down her goals. She wanted to do hairstyles and own a pet shop." This was not the journaling of someone who was planning to commit suicide, she says.

Mack Edwards also finds it difficult to believe Sherokee would commit suicide. "One of two things happened that day," he insists. "Either the kids had something to do with it, are not telling the truth about what happened. Or, she brought the knife to scare them, maybe make some kind of statement, and she accidently pushed it in." He does believe either scenario is directly related to the "bullying" that Sherokee was experiencing that day—and every day.

Abigail Frazier knew Sherokee "since the day she was born." She sadly admits that she and her best friend Heather have grown apart in the last few years. As Sherokee began a friendship with Heather's daughter April, Abigail began to see Heather in Sherokee, as well as an unhappiness that seemed to take root in Sherokee's childhood. Abigail believes Sherokee accidentally stabbed herself. "She wanted those kids to see and feel what she felt. Maybe, if she let them see what they were doing to her, they would stop, and be friends. I don't think it was suicide."

Sherokee's aunt Samantha also insists Sherokee did not kill herself. She presents a different scenario. "My gut tells me it was not suicide or an accident. I think those kids had a hand in it, somehow. But the police just marked it as 'suicide' and closed the case." Samantha believes the investigators just wanted to close the case as soon as possible. She wonders why Rita and the four witnesses were fingerprinted, but the knife was never dusted for prints.

"I don't believe it was suicide," family friend Amy Duke says flatly. "I don't know what happened, but I think those kids had a hand in it. I heard [from a third party] the coroner said that knife was too deep inside of her body for her to have stabbed herself." It was a rumor that circulated consistently around the adults.

"Kids cannot get away from the bullying, the bad things," an adult family friend, said contemplating Sherokee's generation. "When I was a kid, and you got into a fight or someone was bullying you, you just went home. You'd probably even end up being friends later on." A kid could go home, lick their wounds, and stay away from the torment until they felt better, ready to take it on or ready to call a truce.

Abigail Frazier agrees, musing how "there's no solitude nowadays. Now you can't get away from it. When I was a kid and someone was mean, you just left the situation. Kids can't do that anymore. The bullying, the meanness just continues on Facebook, on Twitter, on this social media." She sighs. "There's just no solitude."

Katie Nichols struggles to understand Sherokee purposely hurting herself, or taking her own life. On one hand, she explains, Sherokee had never voiced any suicidal ideations to her; the closest thing to it was when she had told Katie in a fit of exasperation, "I don't want to be here anymore! Sometimes I could just—pull my hair out I get so mad!" Katie still feels that Sherokee had no place to go to be alone. "She had nowhere to escape." The one place where Sherokee might find solitude was Mankin Park.

Katie is unsure if Sherokee purposely took her own life or if she stabbed herself accidently. "Maybe she didn't really think it was the end. How it would affect everyone. I wonder if it was an 'in the moment' thing." Regardless, she adds, "Sherokee looks down on us every day. She's watching us, seeing how we're all doing." Guilt occasionally bubbles to the surface. "If I could have just called her—why didn't I—

what if—" Katie has done a lot of introspection. "It's all over and done," she says sadly. "Can't go back and fix the past."

Anyone who knew Sherokee agreed on one thing: Sherokee's life was a rocky one from the start.

She bounced from doctor to doctor, was pushed through the revolving doors of the offices of psychiatrists and counselors, through treatments and myriad medications in an effort to quell the anger and sadness in her head and heart.

She was caught up in an education system that pushed her from grade to grade despite failing marks. Although she scored low on both quarterly report cards and standardized tests, she was not held back, nor was she placed in a specialized education classroom. Too many people employed in education will testify how the education system bullies the administration: pass the child and keep your job. Teach to the test and utilize a system that may assist a handful of students while the others fall behind and a small percentage exceed. Never make the school where you work appear to be a "problem school," meaning no student rioting, fights, illegal activities, or anything else that negatively marks the school—like bullying. The education system seems to utilize unrealistic "no bullying" programs created by adults, and too many students do not trust adults nor these programs to keep them safe. Many times, students rely on friends to make them feel safe.

Having and keeping friends was another of Sherokee's struggles. Sherokee did not have the social skills nor the understanding that to have a friend, you had to follow rules set forth in society, and she did not understand the unspoken rules that were part of the teenage vernacular. She believed childish behavior would help get what she wanted, but acted too old for her age when it came to dating. She was caught in that zone of time where she was no longer a baby, but nowhere near being mature.

Sherokee experienced the internal turmoil of children not understanding her, of not having the maturity or wisdom to be able to decipher her behavior and work with her. So, "something had to be done," Abigail says, wiping away tears. "Sherokee had to do something to stop it all."

What exactly happened on September 5, 2015, in Mankin Park is difficult to decipher. Eyewitness testimonies vary. The whole truth will never be known.

CHAPTER 61

Cutting ...

Only days after Sherokee stabbed herself, another drama was playing out. It took place behind closed doors. It was a familiar drama among her peers.

The teen sits alone, slowly unwrapping a razor blade. The mental picture of Sherokee with that kitchen knife, that moment of finding out she was dead, kept playing like a broken video: over and over, the teen could see it, hear it, watch Sherokee dying.

I killed her.

It was my fault. I should have stopped it.

I should have saw...

Handling the blade carefully, turning it over and over in both hands. The pain of losing her, the mental picture of her dying over and over ... too much.

The blade moves quietly, lightly across the skin, leaving in its wake a thin line of bright red blood. Friends call it "cutting." Psychiatry calls it "self mutilation;" either way, it makes the emotional pain go away by replacing it with physical pain. It is like the dam breaks: a deluge of pent-up emotions.

Fear and hurt and pain.

Rushing out and away from the body, following the thin trickle of blood looping a path around the curves of the body and then down, down, until the drop fades to a stop.

The pain in the heart stops because the brain is forced to focus on the pain in the body.

Cutters know exactly how to apply pressure, where on the body to cut, when to begin and where to stop, before it goes too far. Before an emergency room visit is warranted.

Cutters are professionals at this game.

It is so much easier to draw blood than draw tears, especially when people are saying, "don't talk about it."

"Just forget it and move on." That was the advice of so many adults, parents, even Sherokee's classmates.

Try and talk about it, how it feels, only to watch people roll their eyes, turn away, and—at best—hush you. It does not matter who you try to talk to: parents, adults, kids your age, family, friends. So then you cut to numb everything else and then no one understands how physical pain helps. No one understands.

Except for another cutter.

Hiding this secret so well that no one knows of the long history of cutting. And if you tell, others will think you are a freak. Learning to hide the origins of those thin little lines across the body. "Cut myself playing… building… the cat scratched me…" Always so easy to explain.

Cutters know how to hide it.

It was my fault. I should have stopped it.

Imaging Sherokee's face as she drove the knife into her belly… Sherokee's voice … Sherokee's howling in pain…

All stored up inside the heart and refusing to be set free, until the razor lets it out, one light, sharp, drag across the skin. Little bubbles of blood popping up. It hurts, it hurts …

"Don't talk about it."

"Just forget about it."

It was my fault. I should have stopped it.

Fear and hurt and pain.

Friendships lost over her death. Childhood lost. Now, blood lost.

Better to lose blood than something else.

Sitting and watching the little ball of blood rolling down. The trail already drying, flaking off with the flick of a nail.

The internal video of Sherokee's death now momentarily paused, watching the blood instead.

HAS EDUCATION FAILED AT "STOP BULLYING" PROGRAMS?

"She was a strong girl because she held on for so long."
—friend of Sherokee Harriman

"Sherokee had so much potential. That's what's so sad."
—Rita Harriman, Sherokee's
grandmother and legal guardian

CHAPTER 62

Some of peers and family members report Sherokee Harriman was, in part, feeling hopeless due to the school district's lack of protection from bullies. And the bullying has continued: people are, even at this writing, destroying the memorial that has been placed in the park where Sherokee fell. "Even in death," says one student through tears, "they disrespect her." Her mother demands an answer: "Why do they continue to try to hurt her?" Has the education system's "no bullying" programs completely failed students?

According to the Suicide Prevention & Resource Center, suicide is the third-leading cause of death for young people ages 12 to 18. Other factors contribute to suicide, yet, "Bullying is associated with increases in suicide risk in young people who are victims of bullying (and) increases depression and other problems associated with suicide." These statistics encompass both the bullies *and* the children being bullied.[13]

Friends, classmates, and students in other schools who knew Sherokee Harriman personally or even marginally report there are in-house programs to report bullying at all their schools. They are also quick to explain why students do not trust the programs: "They [the administration] don't do anything" when bullying is reported and, "If you report, then you are [called] a snitch [by other students]" creating

---

13. www.sptsusa.org

more problems for the students who need and want to report. "So, it's not worth it," one bullied student says blatantly.

Sherokee's mother, Heather, calls the "Zero Tolerance for Bullying" program in their school district "a joke." Heather explains she assisted Sherokee in completing "bully reports" in both junior high and high school, supporting her with long talks and attempts at follow up. They completed one report in the beginning of Sherokee's high school year. The report never went through the system because Sherokee was already in her grave when the bright orange form reached administration.

Sherokee's friend, Taylor Geffre, can tell horror stories of how Taylor herself was treated by students when she attended Stewart's Creek Middle School in Smyrna, Tennessee. In eighth grade she began having suicidal thoughts. "I had no friends, I didn't feel like the teachers or anyone was there to help me." Taylor endured hateful comments, nasty notes, and perceived negative treatment received from both students and staff. When she made second chair in the school band, she asked the band director what kept her from scoring first chair. "Because you're not as good as you think you are," she says she was told. To her mother, the director said curtly, "If she doesn't like how I run my class, she can get out." The tone of the responses hurt her deeply, destroying the only escape Taylor had from the nasty taunts she was enduring outside of the band hall.

A clinical diagnosis and treatment for bipolar and anxiety disorders, as well as a transfer to Holloway High School "saved my life," she says. "Schools should have smaller classes. Teachers should be educated on bipolar disorder. People need to understand 'bipolar.'" She recalls students calling her "Psycho Girl" and "Crazy Girl" because they did not understand her behavior.

These are opinions of a handful of students and parents in anguish, but one student in fear of walking the school hallways and one parent let down by the education system is far too many. Despite the "No Bully Zone" and similar programs, the system appears to be failing both students who feel unsafe in the school and the students who are bullies. Why?

One of the problems that could be preventing success of "Stop Bullying" school programs is lack of educational funding. According to the U.S. Census in 2013, the United States public school system reported an outstanding debt of $415,238,582. Nearly half of K–12 education funding comes from the state (46 percent).[14]

A 2016 study has revealed:

- At least 31 states provided less state funding per student in the 2014 school year than in the 2008 school year. In at least 15 states, the cuts exceeded 10 percent.

- Since 2012, local school districts have restored some of the 351,000 jobs lost during a 2008 budget cut, but still are down 297,000 jobs.

- The number of public K–12 teachers and other school workers has fallen by 297,000 since 2008 while the number of students has *risen* by about 804,000.

- In 31 states, total state funding per student was lower in the 2014 school year than in the 2008 school year, before the recession took hold.[15]

The funding to create and keep "safe school" programs is nearly impossible in a system scrambling to afford the most basic supplies while meeting all budget demands. "We have to pay for so many classroom supplies out of our own pockets because of budget cuts," says one Nashville,

---

14. Census Bureau, "Public Elementary-Secondary Education Finance Report, "2013 data," released 2016.

15. Center on Budget and Policy Priorities, "Most states have cut school funding, and some continue cutting." Jan. 25, 2016. Albares, Leachman, et.al. cbpp.org.

Tennessee, high school teacher. "How are they going to find money to keep a new program running?"

In October 2010, there were allegations that the LaVergne high school principal harassed and bullied teachers and staff to the point where staff was leaving the school for early retirement or resigning. Ten complaints and grievances were filed; at least 50 other teachers complained but feared coming forward for fear of losing their job. The controversy caused faculty members and parents to attend a Rutherford County School Board meeting in an attempt to resolve the issue. Months later, the school's district attorney found no wrongdoing. The principal has a rating of 1.47 out of possible 5.0 by teacher rating on a website "Ratemyprincipal.com." Whether this principal was guilty or not, the hostility raised by the accusations of bullying was sure to trickle down to students, as modeled by parents, teachers, and staff. "Students who witnessed staff be hurtful to a student were significantly more likely to also witness students being hurtful, be hurtful, or have someone be hurtful to them."[16]

Another potential barrier is what teachers can do versus what the system demands. When it was initially drafted, the No Child Left Behind act of 2001 was a possible solution to education's issues. Like so many attempts at repairing the system, educators and officials are reporting it is failing too many schools. It focuses on tests, an assessment-based accountability that works with a few but leaves too many struggling; the system is now more concerned with teaching to a standard rather than combining compassion, education, and social etiquette in lesson plans, adjusting each to assist the learning curves.

In the end, students suffer the most.

---

16. Interview with Nancy Willard, M.S. Special Education, J.D. on May 21, 2016

How does the education system create "stop bullying" programs that meet faculty, students, and parents' goals for a safe school environment while fitting the budget, with a place in the overall curriculum? The effort cannot be deemed impossible or useless. Programs cannot be "one size fits all." One program alone cannot be expected to put a stop to all bullying. Programs need to be respected, fair, and firm.

One potential program would create dialogue between the bullied and the bullies that is monitored by a respected adult. Rather than hearing an adult's lecture, children would be listening to their peers. Such a program would allow the bullied student to express feelings, to ask the bully "why?" Then the bully would be allowed to do the same. If it is a group of bullies, allow them to have open communication together, asking the same question of one another and discussing why they are being hurtful. Valuable lessons would be learned in such a program: good communication, understanding oneself, understanding others, and respect. Will it work with all students? It would be a start. What is the cost? It is the same as for all programs: time and money are needed, but the return on investment is worth trying.

"The recent NAS [National Academy of Science] report indicates that the zero tolerance approach to bullying prevention is not effective," reports Nancy Willard, an author, education specialist, and director of Embrace Civility in the Digital Age. "But a disciplinary approach—rules, staff supervision, tell students, investigate, impose consequences—is exactly what is recommend(ed) for statutes and policies, and what the federal partnership recommends for staff development."

Educational organizations and administration, parents, and staff have their opinions on how to stop bullying in the schools. Perhaps it is time to share the problem-solving with students.

One of Sherokee's friends believes education for instructors and staff about mental health would help. Another believes "we need to get the Bible back in the schools." Most of Sherokee's family members believe bullying should be declared a criminal offense. As with every problem, each person has a solution.

It is far too late for students like Sherokee Harriman and the kids who did bully her; somewhere along the path they all fell through the cracks into the mix of programs, budget demands, and educational system requirements. They slipped through to face a lifetime of remorse and self-blame, or to fall dead in the grass at the tender age of 14.

CHAPTER 63

There are arguments against vigils and the other special recognitions that are held when a child commits suicide, because some feel these events can send the wrong messages: that the sole answer for bully victims is suicide, and that students with suicidal ideations may believe that killing themselves will finally make them popular, whether heroes or martyrs. The kids who feel lost, have no recognition or ties to their community, learn they can be remembered and treasured: all they have to do is take their own life. Yet the dramatic memorials continue.

A balloon release for family and friends had been scheduled in Sherokee's honor from Mankin Park, and Heather and her family were there to prepare. One of the boys who had witnessed Sherokee stab herself came strolling up to the park.

Sherokee had been in her grave for a week. Heather saw the boy enter the park and, trying to hold back, she approached him. She pointed to the group of busy people who were inflating balloons. "You have no business here," she told him.

"Well, uh, I'm in the back of the park," he mumbled, staring at the toe of his shoe. He chanced a look at her.

"You didn't even try to help her," Heather seethed, her brown eyes cutting into his.

"It...it just happened so fast..."

"How dare you come back here!"

"I couldn't even—"

"How dare you! You killed her!"

The boy ducked his head and shambled out, trying not to glance over at the people who stared at him from the pavilion.

"Poor guy left a little on the scared side," Heather would remember later.

Sherokee had been gone a month. It brought comfort to Heather to visit what she calls "Sherokee's pole," the post that has been decorated in pink at Mankin Park. She was visiting the day when she saw Alec Seether at the park. He was there with another boy. Heather recalls what happened next.

Trying not to let tears flood her eyes, she approached Alec. He looked at her then quickly looked away.

"Alec," Heather said, "you told her you would have her back if she was being bullied. You told her!"

Alec looked at the ground.

"Why didn't you have her back that day when she—when Allie was running her mouth! How could you have just sat there and not tried to stop it! Why didn't you just break up with Allie before you all got to the park!"

Heather recalls Alec shrugging and that he could not meet her eyes. "I don't know."

She stared at him for a few seconds, then turned to walk back to the pole, lighting another cigarette. Alec returned to stand with his friend, then he left the park. He did not look back.

To this day, Alec berates himself on social media for not being a good person, apologizing profusely for hurting people.

And still, for all that had already happened, there was more pain to come.

SEXTING

"'Sexting' is the exchange of sexually explicit text messages, including photographs, via cell phone." (United States v. Broxmeyer, 2010 U.S. App. (2d Cir. 2010)

CHAPTER 64

Heather was scrolling through Sherokce's cell phone messages in an attempt to locate any information tying her daughter to the bullies who, in Heather's eyes, were responsible for her youngest child's death. One of the messages stopped her cold. With shaking hands, she scrolled through the messages.

The messages were from Timothy Ashbury, the "older man" Sherokee had dated in 2014. What Heather saw made her scream for Mike.

Timothy had taken photos of his penis and scrotum area with his cell phone camera, then texted them to Sherokee. He was requesting she take photos of her own nude body to send to him.

Heather shouted for Mike, and together they notified police.

Timothy Albert Ashbury was picked up by LaVergne police officers and interviewed on October 15, 2015. He admitted to having sent Sherokee the photographs and yes, he requested she do the same. Having just turned 20 years old at the time of arrest, Timothy was charged with two felony counts of especially aggravated sexual exploitation of a minor and one count of soliciting sexual exploitation of a minor. Timothy was jailed in Rutherford County and bond was set at $250,000.

On his public webpage, Timothy wrote of committing a prior sexual assault in his youth. He was with a babysitter and another girl of undetermined age. This babysitter, he wrote, was constantly harassing and torturing him, even when he was innocent of any wrongdoing. Out of curiosity, when he was up late, he snuck into a room to fondle a girl's breasts as the girl slept. The girl told their babysitter, who put him in "time out" and notified authorities.

He says now that he meant no harm. Having no mother figure nor sisters in his life, he was just curious about the female body.

Timothy writes of a difficult childhood with an alcoholic father. He was bounced from home to home until the sexual assault landed him in foster care. He reports he was adopted by the Ashbury's, resulting in what looked like a happy ending.

The website, and all of Timothy's social media, was shut down shortly after this discovery was made public.[17]

Those who knew Timothy report he was not as popular as he imagined. Timothy could not be trusted; collectively, they reported he was a thief and a liar, and he tended to disappear when people were looking to kick his ass as payback.

He had his own band and was telling people he was working in music production, when he was arrested. A self-reported famous person who claimed he was popular across the globe, Timothy posted numerous videos of himself playing his guitar, as well as one with a friend and himself giggling and acting silly into the camera. But no one was laughing when his court date was set for November 2.

"Justice for Sherokee," her family called it.

But the investigators found a message on Sherokee's cell phone from Sherokee to Timothy, requesting he send pictures of his penis to her cell phone. After her request, she added "JK" (for "just kidding").

"I didn't scroll far enough," Heather explains, "to see that she did that." She considers it all. "I mean, she was

---

17. The website and all of Timothy's social media was shut down shortly after this discovery was made public by this author on examiner.com's Nashville True

thirteen, she was curious. Still, he was 18. He shoulda never done it in the first place." She is quick to snap, "but my daughter wasn't a ho-bag!"

In November 2015, Timothy went before a judge and was sentenced to four month's probation. He was released from jail several weeks later.

"Four month's probation!" Mike was in anguish over the sentence. "Yeah, she asked for the pictures, *but he was an adult.*"

Timothy's best friend discusses the incident honestly. He does not believe Timothy would have sent the pictures at random or without at least one request. Timothy had many problems resulting from a bad childhood, but he is not a sexual predator, the friend insists.

"Let's just say he would never have done it if he wasn't dragged into it, somehow. Timothy makes horrible decisions that hurt himself, but he was not a person who would randomly send pornographic photos or even send them without provocation or suggestion. I think there's more to [the case] than what's been made public," the friend says. No doubt, the friend laments, Timothy Ashbury did send the pictures upon request, something he never should have done. Did Sherokee exchange nude pictures? "I don't know," the friend responds. "I do know two people who knew her well, who I trust, and they say she did not. I tend to believe that."

One of Sherokee's most trusted friends considers if Sherokee did take part in the sexting. "She wasn't completely innocent, you know." They knew each other well enough to know if the other was sexually active. "I think she was sexually active in her mind," the friend says. Otherwise, there was kissing, perhaps some heavy petting. Heather had laid down the rules as to what her daughters were old enough to be doing with boys, says the friend, and Sherokee loved and respected her mother. Still, she was a budding teenager who longed for affection and true love with a boy. "Besides," Sherokee's friend says frankly, "there wasn't any place for them to go to have sex."

CHAPTER 65

Timothy met with this author to sip drinks in a coffee shop and to talk about his arrest, the charges, and Sherokee Harriman. The topic of his sending her nude photos on his cell phone is discussed.

He admits wrongdoing and wishes he could apologize, face to face, to Sherokee's family. "I liked them," he says now. "And she was a sweet girl. A good friend."

"Why do you think her family is so angry, working to get you a harsher sentence?"

"Maybe her family just needs someone to get angry at, someone to blame [for her death]," Timothy wonders.

"Did you know she was only thirteen?"

"No!" he answers blatantly.

"How would you not know?"

"She told me she was older," he insists. "And her build, her personality— she did not look or act thirteen. She looked like she was eighteen." The author wonders how, if Timothy attended Sherokee's birthday parties, he did not know her age.

A now twenty-year-old Timothy shifts his weight, looks down into his cup. Then, again, he looks the interviewer in the eyes. "I swear, I did not know she was that young. I swear it."

Later he would recant as his life spiraled out of control.

CHAPTER 66

On November 7, 2015, a small group of people huddle in their jackets and smoke cigarettes. It was dark at 5 p.m. now, and the darkness makes it seem colder than the fifty degrees as forecast. The group is celebrating Sherokee's life and her fifteenth birthday in Mankin Park, under the pavilion and near her memorial.

Pizza slices are handed out on cheerful birthday-themed paper plates, along with soft drinks. A few teens gather at a table to chatter about their friend, Sherokee: how she loved to swim, window shop in the mall, and play games. She always seemed to have a different boyfriend, and she was always asking her friends to try a new hairstyle.

Delicious slices of cake are handed around. One minute, friends and family members are somber, the next they are laughing and joking. Cigarettes seem to be a mainstay with the adults. Children play on the swing set where Sherokee had sat alone that September 5th. Loved ones perch on the very benches where the teens had lounged just prior to the fateful encounter.

A visitor's log, created from a spiral notebook, is passed around for signatures and messages. "I don't know what to write," one of Sherokee's friends whispers. Tapping the pen, she fights back tears.

Finally, Heather opens a package of balloons and uses a pump to inflate them. The balloons have a light inside of them, creating warm globes in the chilly, dark air.

Sherokee's best friend Katie proudly shows a box to a visitor; originally made to hold a wristwatch, the box is now covered in pink glitter. She shows a tiny rock on which she had carefully drawn a red heart, a friendship bracelet, and a few more handmade trinkets of love. "I made these for Sherokee," she says. "For her birthday."

Shyloe wears a bracelet and necklace of beads that a grief counselor helped her create. She is proud of this jewelry. The beads spell out her sister's first name.

One by one, Sherokee's friends finally join Heather to slowly make their way to Sherokee's makeshift memorial pole. They hold the lighted balloons that bob in the light wind.

"I hate this part," Mike confides, tears in his eyes.

Rather than join those at the memorial, one of Sherokee's friends turns his face away, listening instead to music at the park bench. Heather and the young people spend a few minutes at the memorial, talking and not talking, staring at the flowers and ribbons. Their new balloons are tied in place.

When the few return, the young people take a table and the topic turns to suicide. One of them, not yet 20, admits to taking a handful of pills in the not-so-distant past, only to be discovered by a family member and rushed to the hospital. The girl had grown weary of high school bullying. The other youngsters discuss how so many of their friends, and themselves, have either attempted, or seriously considered, taking their own life. It is a familiar topic which shocks none of them, and all of them have a personal story. They are all under the age of fifteen.

Soon everyone disperses: there is homework and chores to do, another day to start tomorrow.

The young people walk away from the park after hugs and waves of goodbye. Tomorrow will bring more challenges, more anguish, yet these issues are a part of the everyday lives of young people not old enough to take a driver's education course. "Jesus," a visitor exclaims in disbelief to one of the parents, "these are *kids*. Little kids!"

The parent just solemnly nods.

KIDS THESE DAYS

"If Sherokee can help save one life, she did what she was supposed to do here on earth. I think God put her here to bring awareness to help."

—Amy Duke, family friend

CHAPTER 67

Sherokee's friends and family want people who did not know Sherokee to see her as more than a headline. They also want people to understand just how tough life can be for young people.

This chapter is a collection of considerations that may help the reader begin to understand Sherokee's many challenges and her actions. These are not excuses or answers: just things to think about.

A survivor speaks

B. is a stunningly pretty girl at 14. She knew Sherokee and bullying in middle school. Today, she looks like the girl other teens would admire, with sparkling eyes, a wide smile, and long, thick hair. But in the seventh grade, she wore her hair very short, and other kids called her "the boy" and spread rumors about her sexuality, which they knew nothing about.

Where once she could never enjoy school because of bullying, B. is now preparing for college; she excels at science. She can speak with the introspection of a survivor. Of school bullying programs, she says, "The schools don't do enough; they need to do more. Bullying is not the answer to anything. People bully because they're not satisfied with themselves. I want to ask bullies: imagine if you were being bullied? [Sherokee's death] was a terrible thing. No one should go through that."

Sexuality and bullying

At one time in history, not so very long ago, GLBTQ[18] students were considered mentally ill based on their sexual identity, making them pariahs in the school hallways. Such stigma persists today.

Today, with the rising awareness and legal changes bringing sexual orientation and gender identification to the forefront, many high school students are coming out and declaring their sexual orientation or are voicing their support of those who are coming out. Of course, there are detractors, and profane insults still exist.

In the 1950s, girls were forbidden to discuss sex in high school, and the "tramps" or "sluts" were easily called out and the target of scornful gossip. Today, underage pregnancy or sexual activity is more acknowledged if not accepted: television has created "reality" shows based on the lives of unwed pregnant teens, and high schools have become more realistic in their advising students about the responsibilities of being sexually active.

According to the Centers for Disease Control and Prevention, almost 400,000 girls aged 15 to 19 gave birth in 2010, or 34 per 1,000 girls. Less than 40 years ago, a pregnant teen was "sent off" to a home for unwed mothers or to an out-of-town family member, and the situation was discussed in hushed tones. In 2017, things are very different, with special accommodations such as in-school day cares provided in high schools and schools created specifically for pregnant teens.

---

18. Acronym for Gay, Lesbian, Bisexual, Transgendered, Questioning

Still, despite progressive programs, there is shaming and bullying, especially of girls, regarding sexuality. Sherokee was called a "ho," and she was subjected to insults about her body that were very damaging to her self-esteem.

The legal definition of bullying

As of July 2015, all fifty states in the United States had a bullying law, although twenty-two of those states' laws did not include cyber bullying. Wisconsin and Alaska laws do not include electronic harassment. Sixteen states have a criminal sanction, while forty-four states include a school sanction. Montana is the only state that does not require schools to have bullying as part of their policies. Only fourteen states consider off-campus behavior.

Tennessee, Sherokee's home state, has adopted a bill which includes cyber bullying, electronic harassment, criminal and school sanctions, a school policy, and the law encompasses off campus behaviors. Quoting from the Tennessee Code Ann. § 49-6-1014 (2012) 49-6-1014:

(1) A safe and civil environment is necessary for students to learn and achieve high academic standards;

(2) Harassment, intimidation, bullying or cyber-bullying, like other disruptive or violent behavior, is conduct that disrupts a student's ability to learn and a school's ability to educate its students in a safe environment;

The TN Code § 49-6-4502 (2014) defines "Harassment, intimidation or bullying" as "any act that substantially interferes with a student's educational benefits, opportunities or performance." The act may occur "on school grounds, at any school-sponsored activity, on school- provided equipment or transportation or at any official school bus stop."

This includes:

(ii) Knowingly placing a student or students in reasonable fear of physical harm to the student or damage to the student's property;

(iii) Causing emotional distress to a student or students; or

(iv) Creating a hostile educational environment.

Violators of such acts can be charged with a misdemeanor (up to 1 year in prison and a $2,500 fine) for making threats "online as well as certain in- stances of cyberharassment."

What is cyberbullying?

Nancy Willard, M.S., J.D. holds an M.S. in Special Education with a focus on students with emotional challenges. Her background includes law, technology in schools, and teaching emotionally challenged students,. In the 2000s, Willard began to focus her studies on digital risks for young people. Willard authored the first book ever published on cyberbullying, *Cyberbullying and Cyberthreats* (Research Press, 2007). Since 2010, her work has shifted to focusing more on the overall issues of bullying and other hurtful behavior. Willard shares her insight with others in an effort to assist young people. "The difference between bantering/teasing and bullying is that bantering/teasing is basically done in fun—bullying is not. However, there are huge problems in the area of trying to define bullying."

Willard says there are three definitions of bullying:

1. The academic definition: intentional, repeated, imbalance of power. The original concept of imbalance of power was that the target could not get this to stop. But somehow this shifted to an assessment of various characteristics of the young people involved—popularity or physical strength, for example. This is not objective, is entirely confusing, and does not appear to be how young people think—and the academics keep using this definition.

2. The statutory definition: to be specific, the 50 different statutory definitions, on per state. Some of these are grounded

in case law related to discriminatory harassment and free speech. A common definition is "intentional hurtful behavior that is persistent or pervasive that has caused severe distress and is interfering with a student's ability to learn." However, some of the statutory language is exceptionally vague.

3. The common definition: Someone was hurtful.

At present, no federal law directly addresses bullying. In some cases, bullying overlaps with discriminatory harassment which is covered under federal civil rights laws enforced by the U.S. Department of Education and the U.S. Department of Justice. No matter what label is used (bullying, hazing, or teasing), schools are obligated by these laws to address conduct that is: Severe, pervasive or persistent, creates a hostile environment at school... sufficiently serious and/or based on a student's race, color, national origin, sex, disability, or religion.

What is bullicide?
What measures can officials use to determine if the bullying did, in fact, cause someone to commit suicide? Is bullying still to blame for the suicide if the victim also had mental health issues, a weak family structure, a learning disability, or any combination of these challenges? Even if it is determined the bullying was "the last straw," how is that punishable? Lastly, is "causing" a suicide considered murder?

The Legal Information Institute defines "murder" this way:

Murder occurs when one human being unlawfully kills another human being. The precise legal definition of murder varies by jurisdiction. Most states distinguish between different degrees of murder. Some other states base their murder laws on the modern penal code. (retrieved 10-29-2015 from www.law.cornell.edu)

Tennessee Penal Code 39-13-202 defines

- First Degree Murder as "premeditated and intentional."

- Second Degree Murder (39-13-210) is "knowingly killing of another."

- Voluntary Manslaughter (39-13-211) "is the intentional or knowing killing of another in a state of passion produced by adequate provocation sufficient to lead a reasonable person to act in an irrational manner."

In bullying, any of these charges is difficult if not impossible to prove. Even "Assisted Suicide" (39-13-216) has factors that must be met in order to charge the perpetrator with this Class D Felony:

Assisted suicide.

(a) A person commits the offense of assisted suicide who:

(1) Intentionally provides another person *with the means by which such person directly and intentionally brings about such person's own death*; or

(2*) Intentionally participates* in a physical act by which another person directly and intentionally brings about such person's own death; and

(3) *Provides the means* or participates in the physical act with:

(A) *Actual knowledge* that the other person intends to bring about such person's own death; and

(B) *The clear intent* that the other person bring about such person's own death.

(From the Tennessee Penal Code. Italics by the author)

How do these factors relate to Sherokee?

As the director of the Center for Safe and Responsible Internet Use, Nancy Willard has insights into states that require school reports and work she has completed on studies of student-reported bullying.

"Principals most often refuse to label incidents 'bullying.' They do not want the black mark of filing the report. So now they do a diligent investigation and conclude it is not bullying." The more incidents a school has, Willard says, the more likely it will be labeled as a "bad" school. This is considered a reflection of the principal, the executive staff, and the district.

In Sherokee Harriman's case, Willard explains, "The reason she was bullied all along and failing in school is that when stressed, she triggered." Her peers found her an easy target and fun to bully, "because she would overreact. The trauma primed her brain to overreact to danger or threat. That is what the brain naturally does, but much more if a kid has experienced early trauma." Willard finds Sherokee's case, and others like it, "not entirely a history of bullying that caused her to overreact in this [accident/suicide]. The ongoing bullying was a *component*. This was chronic trauma on top of preexisting trauma."

Willard wants people to understand Sherokee's story is not a new one, nor will it be the last for so many like her: preexisting trauma like sexual assault, a house fire, or losing a beloved family member, sets the course and tone. New traumas—mental illness, family dynamics, bullying—exacerbate the course and tone. Trying to breathe under all of this baggage, a child may just give up the struggle. Others learn coping skills and slog forward.

The National Center for Injury Prevention and Control's Division of Violence Prevention released the results of a study on the "Relationship Between Bullying and Suicide" (2014). While the study revealed bullying behavior and suicide-related behavior are closely related, it also revealed, "We don't know if bullying directly causes suicidal behavior… involvement with bullying, along with other risk factors, increases the chance of suicide-related behavior."

The research revealed the bullies, the victim, and the witnesses to the bullying behavior all have "serious and long-lasting negative consequences" on youth. Witnesses report feelings of helplessness and no sense of connectedness to the schools.[19] The "ripple effect of crime" is in effect as the bullying behavior will circumvent through all involved.

Social media, personal computers, and cell phones are easy to blame for problems because they are machines and cannot defend themselves. Anything new—technology, trends, and the like—bring both bad and good into our lives. And people like to believe there is someone or something to blame.

"What is wrong with kids these days?" is a familiar mantra among adults. But as the ancient Roman emperor Marcus Aurelius (26 April 121 – 17 March 180 AD) wrote, "Life is neither good nor evil, but only a place for good and evil." "These days" have actually been going on since the beginning of time, for every generation has had its woes: a teenager in ancient Greece was lucky to see his twentieth birthday due to disease and living conditions. During the Industrial Revolution, children as young as six went to work in factories and coal mines; preschoolers labored on farms and in the home. In the 1950s, "duck and cover" was a very frightening school program, teaching children to hide under their desks should an atomic bomb be dropped. There are generations who can share how they spent their teenaged years in concentration camps, or feared their neighbor may be a Communist spy, or were made to fear a terrorist attack, or were drafted into war before they were old enough to order a beer. Problems facing young people are not new.

It is not just the age we live in, but the perpetual turbulence of being caught between child- and adulthood; the confusing

---

19. Page 7 of the report.

messages from peers, adults, the government, and the world; and, of course, hormones now raging through the physical and mental body, all exacerbated by the unnatural chemicals in our food and drink. The problems, fears, and internal wars have not changed, only the environment in which they are surrounded.

How real is "Bullycide"?

I hate some people
—September 1, 2013, Facebook post by Sherokee Harriman

I feel loved by my family and friends
—September 9, 2013, Facebook post by Sherokee Harriman

CHAPTER 68

In 1997, a thirteen-year-old girl in Allentown, England, unwittingly put the word *bullicide* onto the map. Living in a working-class neighborhood a little over 100 miles from London, Kelly Yeomans purposely overdosed on her mother's pain medication, alone in her bedroom as her family slept. She took 13 times the minimal lethal dose of the drug.

According to court testimony, Kelly was harassed and bullied incessantly, usually about her weight. Kelly's glasses had been broken, her new shoes and book bag tossed into a Dumpster, and she actually bore bruises from being stabbed with pencils. Bullying students purposely destroyed her school lunches. Just prior to her suicide, a group of school kids pelted the Yeoman's home with food, shouting taunts. They left pornographic pictures in the mailbox. One boy admitted on the stand that Kelly was called "fatty," "bastard," and "tramp." The Yeomans reported Kelly had tried to shoulder on despite multiple setbacks. Finally, she had enough.

Kelly reportedly had problems at home and with depression. She had actually said she was going to take her own life just prior to her overdose. A neighbor told the media the special needs girl was mistreated at home.

On January 14, 2010, Phoebe Prince was found in her home where she had hanged herself with a scarf that was a gift from her sister. The media reported it as a suicide caused by bullying. At the time, the media failed to report Phoebe's history of drug abuse, her self-mutilation, or her depression. She often had riffs with other girls over "stealing" boyfriends. She had a history of attempting suicide. She penned school papers on missing her father and how she understood why young people would self-mutilate. A few girls at school began name-calling and taunting, angry at Phoebe for dating "their" boyfriends. By the time the media learned of her history, her story was old news; the 15-year-old girl's story had dropped from the front pages.

Rebecca Sedwick made national headlines when the Lakeland, Florida, girl jumped to her death: she was just twelve years old. Rebecca threw herself off a high tower at a cement plant where she would often escape to be alone. Law enforcement officials and her family blamed bullying before an investigation revealed so many additional stressors. The online messages her classmates sent her, calling her names such as "ho" and "ugly" were polarizing and publically revealed without explanation. The sheriff announced in a public statement, "Rebecca was a very fragile child. Rebecca's wagon was already pretty heavily burdened with bricks... what the bullies did is that they continued to stack bricks on an already overloaded wagon, till finally it broke."[20] Later, an investigation by an unbiased nonprofit organization revealed Rebecca was suffering depression, her relationship with her father was deteriorating, and she was fighting with her mother and stepfather. She had self-mutilated. Like so many other girls, she had an online "boyfriend," but he had just cut ties to her. Rebecca had been previously hospitalized for suicidal ideations. She had researched the lethal dosage of over-the-counter pills. Her diary reports she felt suicidal. Throughout school, bullies told Rebecca to "go drink bleach and kill yourself;" "you

---

20. Associated Press, 2014

should die;" and "nobody likes you" in response to her public posting of the desire to kill herself.

Montana Lance was only nine-years-old when he hung himself.[21] Ty Smalley shot himself at 11.[22] Alexis Moore, 15, jumped to her death from a busy overpass. Celina Okwuone took her life at 11.[23] Cassidy Andel was 16 when she hung herself.[24] All of these suicidal children suffered from emotional and physical ailments; were diagnosed with mental illness or emotional disorders; and/or were experiencing serious issues at home and in school. Yet each suicide was publically blamed on bullying.

Blaming bullying as the *sole purpose* of suicide is not realistic. It perpetuates the false notion that "suicide is a natural response to being bullied…has the dangerous potential to both normalize the response and can create 'copycat' behavior." It encourages sensationalized reporting and spreads false information. The wrong people are blamed and punished. Ultimately, the attention is not on true suicidal risk factors, such as mental illness, family dysfunction, etc. The report "Relationship Between Bullying and Suicide," suggests punishment for bullying is important, but the best practice is to move past the punishment to "set the tone for lasting prevention."

"The Relationship Between Bullying and Suicide" reveals youth who bully, the victims of bullying, and those who witness bullying but take no action are *all* at high-risk

21.   Estate of Montana Lance, Jason Lance, Deborah Lance v. Lewisville Independent School District, No. 12-41139; filed 02/28/2014
22.   David & Tina Long v. Murray County School District, and Gina Linder, etc., Civil Action No. 4:10-CV-00015-HLM, filed 12/20.2011
23.   A. Marra, "Suicide victim was bright and liked…" *Palm Beach Post*, May 29, 2010.
24.   "Family of Cassidy Andel releases open letter," WDAY AM 970, legacy.wday.com, November 17, 2010.

for suicide-related behavior, including anxiety, depression, substance abuse, and poor performance in school (low grades, poor attendance, somatic symptoms, and little if any social functioning).

But to prove "suicide by bullying," the definition and elements of the crime must be determined. All of the issues must be examined. We must consider the totality of circumstances rather than blame one factor. Lastly, the media and the caregivers need to report the entire story rather than provide a knee-jerk reaction that make lurid headlines.

While the media coverage focuses on the blame and criminal justice focuses on intervention, researchers are focusing on evidence, facts, and preventative methods to assist youths in the future.

That September 2015 afternoon in Mankin Park, the argument between teens was not the singular reason, but a variable in Sherokee's suicide. Perhaps Sherokee Harriman had enough of the world that she could not deal with the hateful messages heaped upon her already weary shoulders. Rather than leave the park when the name-calling began, she tried to reason; she fought back as a last resort. Still, maybe if she did return, they could be friends. If not, well then, she would scare them. And to scare them, she would show them how much she hurt and how seriously they had hurt her.

And they would hurt just as badly and just as long as she had been hurt, even after she was gone.

One of Sherokee's friends says now, "If they hadn't have hit that last button, maybe [Sherokee] wouldn't have done it. If they weren't even there that day... if they hadn't been mean. But they didn't know her, didn't know she had a knife..."

"She was a strong girl because she held on for so long," says a family friend. "She held on for so long, but bullying got the best of her."

As with so many things in her life, Sherokee Harriman may have simply misjudged. Like so many times before, she handled the situation wrong. Knives are more dangerous than she imagined. But the other teens also handled the situations incorrectly. Their words were also much more dangerous then they could have dreamed.

AFTERWORD

Y can't I be popular. I feel like I'm a stupid girl
who just wants to be treated right and not get hurt
wherever I go I don't feel like I have a safe place not
school or my house (crying face emoji added)

—Posted by Sherokee Harriman on
Facebook, August 12, 2015

CHAPTER 69

THE AFTERMATH

There is a pole in Mankin Park, La Vergne, Tennessee, near the spot where Sherokee Rose Harriman fell after stabbing herself. It is decorated with notes, flowers, balloons, and streamers—all pink. The family has had to repair the memorial several times due to unknown persons vandalizing it by tearing up notes, popping balloons, and stealing candles and mementos.

In death, Sherokee received one more report in her school file, this time at LaVergne High School. It is a withdrawal form, accompanied by her student schedule. Across the form in handwriting is the note:

Deceased 9-5-15

Sherokee's family has not publically revealed the location of her grave for fear it will be vandalized. Only close family members know where she is buried.

Mack continues to reside in Ohio. He has several children, some living in Ohio. He wishes things could have been different, most of all that he could have met Sherokee in life. He does believe bullying played a role in her death, and this angers him. "She was too sweet, too sweet to be bullied," he says.

Heather and Mike continue to live in Tennessee. Shyloe lives with them, sleeping in the same bedroom she shared with her sister. She recalls Sherokee "fixing my hair, doing my makeup. I looked pretty."

Sherokee's grandmother and legal guardian, Rita Harriman, still lives with Heather, Mike, and Shyloe. All admit they still bicker and argue.

"We have our good days and our bad days," Mike says of his family's survival after Sherokee's death. They love showing Sherokee's writing, her pictures, and her bedroom to guests. Sherokee's bedroom walls are still adorned with magazine photos of teenage musicians and actors. Next to the pictures of the cute adolescent boys, she taped up magazine pages of beauty tips and makeup tricks.

One of Sherokee's maternal uncles, CJ, continues to promote Stand Against Bullying Tennessee. He and his wife have spent thousands of dollars in promoting and preparing for the organization to achieve legal nonprofit status.

Of the "bullies" at Mankin Park that day, some are still friends; others have cut ties with one another.

- A few weeks after Sherokee's death, one of the kids accused of bullying Sherokee announced he/she "just want to put it all behind (them) and go on with life." (Indeterminate pronouns are used here to protect the young peoples' identities.)

- Another accused bully confided he/she felt suicidal and lost, with no one to talk to about pain.

- One of the bullies has resorted to self-mutilation again, a problem this person thought he/she had overcome.

- Still another insists he/she did not cause Sherokee's demise, but will never talk about that day in the park.

- Rumors have it that one of the kids moved away to another state for personal safety; another rumor is that he/she continues to live in the LaVergne area and is being home-schooled. Other kids accuse this student of "killing" Sherokee.

- One of the youth has used Facebook as a forum to express sorrow, regret, and pain.

Only weeks after Sherokee died, Debi and Allie posted pictures of themselves on Facebook: they were going to a special event in Nashville, having fun together, smiling for the camera.

Sherokee's friends find it heart-wrenching to go on without her. They get by, day by day. Some have good support systems. Others carry the burden alone.

- Taylor Geffre is now in college with plans to become a meteorologist. She loves math and science, and her current medication keeps her mental health in check. But no matter where she is in life, Taylor feels guilty for Sherokee's suicide. "I would see on Facebook where she would post about being sad, when her family was posting about her being happy," Taylor confides. "It's just so hard to talk to your family, because you're not sure how they'll react. Will they get mad? Think you're crazy?" She is unsure of the real story that took place that day in Mankin Park, but she feels if it was suicide: Sherokee had a plan, "because you always have a plan when you're going to commit suicide." She says now of Sherokee, "She was a sweet girl. She cared about people. She would even stand up for other kids being bullied."

- Angel Hollenbeck recalls Sherokee with fondness, despite the rift between them that was never resolved. Mutual friends believe Sherokee's death has left Angel feeling guilt for cutting off the friendship for some silly disagreement.

- Katie Nichols feels, toward the end, she was the only real friend Sherokee had left. Sherokee's best friend is preparing to graduate high school. She still wants to be a psychologist. Katie remains wise beyond her years. She is close to Sherokee's family, joining them at memorials and holidays. Katie is one friend of Sherokee's who has never had suicidal ideations.

- As this book was near completion, one of Sherokee's friends and a contributor to this book is in a local hospital. After attempting suicide twice in less than six months, the young teen will next be admitted to a mental health hospital. The youth's family blames bullying. Another of Sherokee's friends had a breakdown and was hospitalized for a short time and was released.

- Timothy Ashbury was placed on probation and is reportedly living with his father and his grandfather. January 2017 found Timothy back in jail for probation violation when he lied about employment. He admits now he knew Sherokee's true age when he sent the nude pictures. He wrote from jail, "Sherokee was 13 yrs. old, and I knew it. I don't care what others say / think." He claims Sherokee wanted his protection, and wanted to join "secret societies" and "the cult." Timothy's letters from his stint in jail are long, garbled, and rambling, with grandiose thoughts of memberships in secret societies and anti-government underground organizations, and he suggests he is privy to conspiracies. He is convinced he has offers from major music labels to produce his music. At this writing, Timothy Ashbury is out of jail after having served his time.

• Mack Edwards discusses Sherokee's death, then breaks down into tears. "All she wanted," Mack sobs uncontrollably, "was a friend. Just a god-damned friend." When he can manage to speak, he takes a deep breath to ask, "Why is that so bad?"

PICTURES

Sherokee Rose Harriman
November 7, 2000 - September 5, 2015

Heather and Mack, Sherokee's biological parents. This photo was taken at Sherokee's funeral, September 2015.

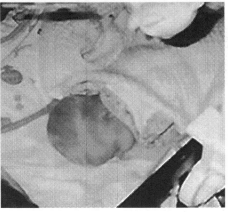

Sherokee, 23 days old. She was a sickly baby.

Sherokee's first picture with her older "Sissy."

Two-year-old Shyloe points to a book for
her one-year-old sister Sherokee.

Sherokee, two years old.

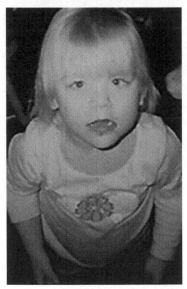

"Sherokee was a sweet baby," says a family
friend, "and I loved her little chubby cheeks."

Sherokee making her "signature sign." She loved the
color pink, hearts, and animals. This is Mack Edwards'
favorite photo of his daughter; he never got to meet
her in person. (photo courtesy Mack Edwards)

Mike Edwards never liked the term "stepfather."
Sherokee and her sister called him "dad." Here he
is with Sherokee at a father-daughter banquet.

Thanksgiving 2010: Sherokee with her maternal grandparents and legal guardians, Joe and Rita Harriman. One person has been cropped out of the photograph to protect their privacy (photo courtesy Loretta Harriman)

Heather poses with her youngest daughter, Sherokee Rose. Sherokee is 12 years old in this photo.

Sherokee and her best friend Katie. "Towards the end
(of her life) I was really Sherokee's
only friend," Katie says now.

Like most girls her age, Sherokee took many
"selfies." She told people on numerous occasions,
"I wish I was popular. I wish I was pretty."

The last picture Katie took of Sherokee. The shirt around her waist was a gift from Katie.

September 2015: Sherokee completed a job application just prior to her death. Her proud daddy snapped this photo of her.

Sherokee loved trying different hairstyles. She dreamed of owning her own hair and nails salon. In one of her last selfies, she sports her new look; she dyed her hair black after she cut it herself.

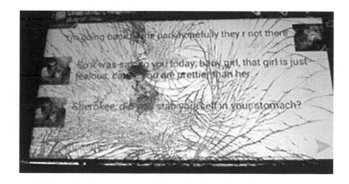

Sherokee's last communication with her loved ones was on this cellular phone at 12:48 p.m. on September 5, 2015: "I'm going back to the park hopefully they r not there" and Heather's text "Sherokee, did you stab yourself in the stomach?"(Author's collection)

Sherokee's Memorial in Mankin Park. She fell
just at the bend of the pathway, near the rail fence.
The pavilion where her alleged bullies sat can be
seen in the background. (Author's collection)

Sherokee's last school picture, 8th grade, 2014.
It now adorns her headstone and appears
with her printed obituary.

Sherokee's headstone. Her parents keep its location private to prevent vandalism. (photo courtesy Loretta Harriman)

Posing with her dog, Lilly. This is the memorial photograph used for social media.

I am a rose / I like to be pretty
I grow in the summer / I am happy
I often grow all day / I sometimes sparkle
I feel special / I am a rose

—Personification Poem by Sherokee Harriman

RESOURCES & REFERENCES

The author wishes to thank Nancy Willard for her insight and information. Ms. Willard is the director of the Center for Safe and Responsible Internet Use. She has over 12 years experience working with at-risk youth and teaching about Web safety in schools. She is also the author of numerous articles and books, including *Cyberbullying and Cyberthreats: Responding to the Challenge of Online Social Aggressors, Threats, and Distress*, and *Cyber-Safe Kids, Cyber-Savvy Teens*. To learn more or to order the books, go to www.internetsafetyproject.org/wiki/center-safe-and-responsible-internet-use. Her blog can be read here: csriu.wordpress.com

Students Against Violence Everywhere (SAVE)
The National Association of Students Against Violence Everywhere (SAVE), Inc. is a public, nonprofit organization that strives to decrease the potential for violence in our schools and communities by promoting meaningful student involvement, education, and service opportunities in efforts to provide safer environments for youth.

Students Against Violence Everywhere
322 Chapanoke Rd # 110
Raleigh, NC 27603
(866) 343-SAVE
info@nationalsave.org
Nationalsave.org

The Society for the Prevention of Teen Suicide offers myriad free programs, including resources for educators. This organization supplies education, support, books, training, and toolkits. Learn more:

www.sptsusa.org
The Society for the Prevention of Teen Suicide
110 West Main Street
Freehold, NJ 07728
(732)410-7900

Crisis hotline for you or someone you know: **1-800-273-8255**

For information on bullying, including definitions, education, responses, and prevention, there is government-sponsored website that includes laws, warning signs, and best practices in response.

www.stopbullying.gov
The U.S. Department of Health & Human Services
200 Independence Avenue S.W.
Washington, D.C. 20201

Embrace Civility in the Digital Age promotes a twenty-first century approach to address bullying and youth risk in the digital age. It promotes positive norms, increases effective skills and resiliency, and encourages young people to be helpful allies who positively intervene when they witness peers being hurt or at risk.
Embrace Civility in the Digital Age
POB 899
Creswell, Oregon 97426
541-566-1145
www.embracecivility.org

Edutopia is a program that shares evidence- and practitioner–based learning strategies empowering the improvement of K–12 education. This includes information and resources on the issue of bullying. Edutopia provides many program ideas, education, videos, suicide prevention information, parents and educator resources, cyber bullying, creating social and emotional learning, diversity and inclusion, and many other resources. The information can be found at: www.edutopia.org

For more information on the bullying laws in your state, go to **cyberbullying.org/Bullying-and-Cyberbullying-Laws. pdf**.

The National Center for Injury Prevention Injury Prevention and Control's Division of Violence Prevention. (2014). "Relationship Between Bullying and Suicide."
Retrieved from http://www.cdc.gov/violenceprevention/pdf/bullying-suicide-translation-final-a.pdf.

For a list of resources on bipolar disorder: **www. medpagetoday.com**.

Families of bipolar children can find educational articles, references, and resources at The Balanced Mind. This is a not-for-profit, family-operated organization; The Balanced Mind Parent Network was born of the needs of parents of children with mood disorders. It provides community for support and guidance.
Depression and Bipolar Support Alliance (DBSA)
ATTN: Balanced Mind Parent Network
55 E. Jackson Blvd., Suite 490
Chicago, IL 60604
(312)642-0049
crisis line: 1-800-273-TALK
info@thebalancedmind.org

www.thebalancedmind.org

The **Depression and Bipolar Support Alliance (DBSA)** provides support, education, assistance, and hope to improve the lives of people with mood disorders:
The Depression and Bipolar Support Alliance
55 E. Jackson Blvd., Suite 490
Chicago, ILL. 60604
1-800-826-3632
www.dbsalliance.org

For a study on fire-starting in juveniles:
Juvenile Firesetting: A research Overview (Kirkpatrick & Putnam, May 2005). Juvenile Justice Bulletin published by The U.S. Department of Justice Office of Juvenile Justice & Delinquency Programs. The online resource may be obtained here:
https://www.ncjrs.gov/pdffiles1/ojjdp/207606.pdf

...and a special thank you to authors Ann Rule and Lois Duncan, who were brave enough to share their stories and wise enough to persevere when others told them it was not possible. Thank you for all you taught me; thank you for being victim's advocates in your work and life. May St. Michael fold you and your loved ones in his wings. Rest easy; we have your six.

ABOUT THE AUTHOR

Judith A. Yates is a criminologist and an award-winning true crime author. Her first book, "The Devil You Know," won Killer Nashville's 2013 Silver Falchion Award for Best True Crime. The book also includes information on crime awareness for young people.

Ms. Yates' resume includes education (including program director for numerous criminal justice departments), the Federal Bureau of Prisons, the Wichita County, Texas Sheriff's Department, retail loss prevention, and employment as a private investigator. She has attended the Federal Law Enforcement Training Centers in Georgia and New Mexico; the Wicklander School of Interview & Interrogation; the W. F. Bolger Academy in Maryland; and a multitude of law-enforcement classes and training courses across the United States.

She lectures and is a consultant on criminal justice issues, including practical crime prevention and safety for children, and has taught crime prevention and domestic violence awareness for over 25 years. Her master's thesis, a study on school violence and bullying as a factor, received critical praise.

Ms. Yates is a freelance journalist who writes for a variety of law enforcement and education publications; her fiction has been published in collegiate magazines. She has appeared on numerous talk shows.

She volunteers on the Tabitha Tuders missing child case in Nashville, Tennessee, with Nashville Peacemakers, and in animal rescue and adoption. She is "mom" to various animals on her family's small farm. Originally from Texas, she currently resides in Kentucky. She has admitted to phobias of clowns, alligators, and dental offices, but not necessarily in that order. She is a self-confessed addict of bottled Coca-Cola, enjoys travel, photography and flea markets, and is a video-gamer.

For More News About Judith A. Yates,
Signup For Our Newsletter:

http://wbp.bz/newsletter

Word-of-mouth is critical to an author's long-term success. If you appreciated this book please leave a review on the Amazon sales page:

http://wbp.bz/btda

ANOTHER GREAT READ FROM WILDBLUE PRESS!

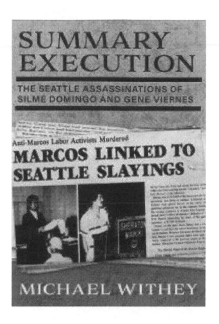

SUMMARY EXECUTION by MICHAEL WITHEY

An incredible true story that reads like an international crime thriller peopled with assassins, political activists, shady FBI informants, murdered witnesses, a tenacious attorney, and a murderous foreign dictator.

"If you have not heard Mike Withey tell the story of the cover-up of the Domingo/Viernes murders, you have not lived."— Vince Warren, Executive Director, Center for Constitutional Rights

http://wbp.bz/se

More True Crime You'll Love From WildBlue Press

RAW DEAL by Gil Valle

RAW DEAL: The Untold Story of the NYPD's "Cannibal Cop" is the memoir of Gil Valle, written with co-author Brian Whitney. It is part the controversial saga of a man who was imprisoned for "thought crimes," and a look into an online world of dark sexuality and violence that most people don't know exists, except maybe in their nightmares.

wbp.bz/rawdeal

BETRAYAL IN BLUE by Burl Barer & Frank C. Girardot Jr.
Adapted from Ken Eurell's shocking personal memoir, plus hundreds of hours of exclusive interviews with the major players, including former international drug lord, Adam Diaz, and Dori Eurell, revealing the truth behind what you won't see in the hit documentary THE SEVEN FIVE.

wbp.bz/bib

THE POLITICS OF MURDER by Margo Nash

"A chilling story about corruption, political power and a stacked judicial system in Massachusetts."–John Ferak, bestselling author of FAILURE OF JUSTICE.

wbp.bz/pom

FAILURE OF JUSTICE by John Ferak

If the dubious efforts of law enforcement that led to the case behind MAKING A MURDERER made you cringe, your skin will crawl at the injustice portrayed in FAILURE OF JUSTICE: A Brutal Murder, An Obsessed Cop, Six Wrongful Convictions. Award-winning journalist and bestselling author John Ferak pursued the story of the Beatrice 6 who were wrongfully accused of the brutal, ritualistic rape and murder of an elderly widow in Beatrice, Nebraska, and then railroaded by law enforcement into prison for a crime they did not commit.

wbp.bz/foj

10108579R00179